THE UNOFFICIAL GUIDE TO WIMBLEDON 2025

SIMON HARRISON

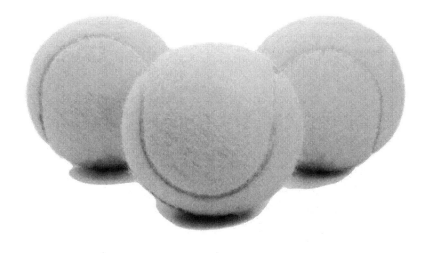

Copyright © 2025 by Simon Harrison

All rights reserved.

No portion of this book may be reproduced in any form without written permission from the publisher or author, except as permitted by U.K. copyright law.

Contents

1. Foreword: A Grand Salute to Wimbledon and the Road   1
   to 2025

2. The Road to SW19   9

3. Setting the Stage   15

4. The Tournament Time Table: Weeks One & Two   23

5. The Early Rounds   28

6. Second Week Showdowns   30

7. The Women's Championship   33

8. The Men's Championship   39

9. Disability Tennis at Wimbledon   45

10. Doubles and Mixed Doubles   50

11. The Juniors and Future Stars   55

12. Men's World Rankings as of March 2025   58

13. Women's Tennis WTA Rankings as of March 2025   60

Foreword: A Grand Salute to Wimbledon and the Road to 2025

It's hard to overstate the magic that surrounds Wimbledon. For over a century and a half, this iconic tournament has been more than just a sporting event—it's a living, breathing piece of tennis history. As we approach the 2025 Championships, there's an electrifying buzz in the air, a sense of anticipation that tingles like the first serve on a dewy morning at the All England Club. Grab a cuppa, settle in, and let's take a leisurely stroll down memory lane before peering eagerly into what promises to be one of the most transformative editions of Wimbledon yet.

A Storied Institution on the Grass

Wimbledon isn't merely a tennis tournament; it's the grand old dame of the sport. From its inception in 1877, when the first championship was held on meticulously manicured grass courts, Wimbledon has stood as the epitome of tennis tradition. Back then, the idea of competitive tennis was still in its infancy, yet even in those early days, something about the pristine lawns, the elegant white attire, and the unspoken rules of conduct set this tournament apart from any other.

The All England Club, nestled in the leafy environs of London, has long been a sanctuary for those who revel in the beauty of the game. Over the decades, Wimbledon has seen legends rise, rivalries intensify, and history being written stroke by stroke. It's a place where past glories mingle with present ambitions—a stage that has seen the likes of Rod Laver, Billie Jean King, Björn Borg, and Martina Navratilova grace its courts. These are names that echo through time, each champion contributing to the rich tapestry of memories that define Wimbledon.

Wimbledon's legacy isn't built solely on the triumphs and trials of its players, though. It's also about the timeless traditions that give the tournament its unmistakable character. Think of the gentle hum of anticipation before the match begins, the aroma of freshly cut grass mingling with that of strawberries and cream, and the strict adherence to etiquette that has remained remarkably intact over the years. It is this blend of reverence for history and the pursuit of sporting excellence that has cemented Wimbledon's esteemed place in the annals of tennis.

The Evolution of Tradition

As much as we cherish the venerable customs of Wimbledon, change is inevitable. The sport of tennis, like any other, must evolve if it is to remain relevant and dynamic. And so, as we edge closer to the 2025 Championships, we find ourselves on the brink of a new era—one that promises to blend time-honoured tradition with cutting-edge innovation.

The narratives swirling around Wimbledon 2025 are as diverse as they are compelling. There's the exciting prospect of witnessing familiar faces return to the grass, veterans who have carved their names into the tournament's storied history, alongside a fresh crop of talents eager to etch their own legacy. The past season has been a rollercoaster of upsets and breakthroughs, and every match on the grass now carries the weight of expectation. There's an underlying hum of excitement—whispers of emerging rivalries, tantalising storylines about comeback kids and dark horses ready to seize their moment in the spotlight.

For many, Wimbledon is a pilgrimage—a destination where one can experience the full spectrum of human endeavour, from heartbreak to triumph. It's where the slow burn of determination meets the explosive energy of a perfectly struck forehand. As we look towards 2025, the narrative is clear: this isn't just another tournament, it's a turning point, a moment where the past and future converge on those sacred courts.

The All England Club: A Testament to Time

The charm of Wimbledon lies as much in its setting as it does in its competition. The All England Club is a masterpiece of tradition and elegance. Walking through its hallowed grounds, one can't help but feel a sense of reverence—a connection to the countless battles fought here over the years. The grand, ivy-clad buildings and the immaculately kept lawns evoke memories of bygone eras, even as modern technology and innovations steadily make their presence felt.

This year, the anticipation is heightened by the announcement of significant changes that will soon become part of the tournament's rich legacy. One of the most talked-about innovations is the complete phasing out of traditional line judges, replaced by an advanced Live Electronic Line Calling system. For many, this marks the end of an era. Those familiar figures in their smart blazers, standing stoically at the baseline and delivering crisp "Out!" calls, will soon be a thing of the past. While it may sting the hearts of tradition purists, the move is a nod to the relentless march of progress.

After extensive testing during previous championships and careful deliberation by the All England Club's board, the verdict is in: the technology is now sufficiently robust to take over. This decision, made in tandem with similar moves by the ATP at other major events, underscores a broader shift in the world of tennis—a move towards consistency and precision. It's a fascinating juxtaposition: on one hand, we have the revered human element that has defined the sport for generations, and on the other, a new digital era where split-second decisions are made by unblinking cameras and computers.

A New Chapter in the Wimbledon Saga

Change, while sometimes unsettling, is an inevitable part of any long-standing tradition. Wimbledon has weathered many storms over the decades—from wars and economic downturns to the occasional controversial decision—and each time, it has emerged stronger, more resilient, and ever more compelling. The narratives leading into Wimbledon 2025 are infused with this same spirit of renewal and reinvention.

For the players, the shift represents both a challenge and an opportunity. Imagine the strategic recalibration required when every call is now subject to the infallibility (or, at times, the unyielding rigidity) of technology. For the fans, it's a promise of a more consistent and arguably fairer game, where the margin for human error is significantly reduced. Yet, there's a bittersweet note to it all—a sense of loss for the charm and unpredictability that only human judgement can bring.

As we stand on the cusp of this new chapter, the atmosphere is charged with a sense of anticipation. There are plenty of questions and debates among enthusiasts: Will the change enhance the flow of the game, or will it rob Wimbledon of a touch of its soul? Can technology truly replicate the nuanced call of a seasoned line judge, whose years of experience lend a certain poetry to the game? While opinions may vary, one thing is clear: Wimbledon 2025 is set to be a landmark event, one that will be remembered for its bold strides into the future, even as it honours its illustrious past.

Anticipation in the Air

It's not just the technological overhaul that has everyone talking. The road to Wimbledon 2025 is paved with rich storylines and dramatic narratives that promise to captivate and entertain. This year has seen some of the most riveting action on the tour, with rising stars and established champions both vying for glory. The 2024 season has set the stage beautifully, with intriguing match-ups, shocking upsets, and awe-inspiring performances that have left fans clamouring for more.

Every season brings its own set of heroes and anti-heroes, and 2025 appears to be no different. With the dust still settling from the previous season's surprising turns, there's a palpable sense that we are about to witness history in the making. The returning champions carry with them not just the weight of expectation, but also the promise of defying the odds once again. Meanwhile, new contenders are hungry to carve out their own niche, to make a mark on the hallowed grass and etch their names alongside the greats.

In the run-up to the Championships, the media is abuzz with speculation and prediction. Talk of potential rivalries, tactical masterclasses, and breakthrough performances fills every conversation—from the stately corridors of the All England Club to the spirited debates in pubs and living rooms across the UK. Fans are busy rewatching classic matches, poring over statistics, and sharing their own predictions, all in a bid to decode the magic that is uniquely Wimbledon.

The Human Element in a Digital Age

At its heart, Wimbledon is about more than just scores and statistics—it's about the human drama that unfolds with every match. The thrill of a match point, the agony of a near miss, and the sheer determination of players pushing beyond their limits are the elements that have defined the tournament over the decades. As we prepare for 2025, these timeless narratives remain as central as ever, even as new technological enhancements reshape the game.

For the purists, the move towards electronic line calling might seem like a cold, impersonal shift—a departure from the tactile, human touch that has characterised the sport for so long. Yet, it's worth remembering that even as we embrace innovation, the soul of Wimbledon remains rooted in the passion and perseverance of its players. The countless hours of training, the sacrifices made in pursuit of excellence, and the raw emotion displayed on court are factors that no machine can replicate. It is this delicate balance between tradition and modernity that makes Wimbledon such a compelling spectacle.

There's a certain charm in imagining how future generations will look back on this pivotal moment. They might recall the day when the familiar voices of the line judges were silenced by the hum of cameras and the whir of computer algorithms—a day when Wimbledon took a bold leap into the future. And yet, as they do, they will also remember the enduring legacy of the tournament: its unwavering commitment to the spirit of tennis, its celebration of human endeavour, and its ability to inspire millions around the globe.

Reflections on a Legacy in the Making

Wimbledon has always been more than just a tennis tournament—it's a mirror reflecting the evolution of the sport and, indeed, of society itself. Over the decades, the Championships have adapted to changes in technology, fashion, and even social norms, all while remaining true to the core values that define it. The anticipation leading into Wimbledon 2025 is tinged with nostalgia for what has been, even as it heralds exciting new possibilities.

The narratives that now swirl around the tournament are rich and varied. There's the story of tradition meeting modernity, of a sport that honours its heritage while boldly stepping into the future. It's the tale of champions defending their legacy against a backdrop of relentless innovation, and of emerging talents eager to challenge the status quo. Whether it's the dramatic comebacks, the nail-biting finishes, or the quiet moments of individual brilliance, Wimbledon continues to capture the imagination of fans around the world.

For many, Wimbledon is a personal journey—a rite of passage that transcends mere competition. It's where dreams are realised and legends are born, where every match is a narrative of hope, struggle, and triumph. As we look ahead to 2025, the excitement is palpable. Every stroke of the racquet, every swing of momentum, and every exultant cheer from the crowd contributes to a legacy that is both timeless and ever-evolving.

The Road Ahead

As we set our sights on Wimbledon 2025, it's impossible not to feel a surge of anticipation. The tournament stands at a crossroads—a juncture where the venerable traditions of the past meet the boundless potential of the future. The decision to embrace electronic line calling, for instance, is emblematic of a broader shift in the world of tennis.

It's a move that underscores the commitment to fairness, precision, and a modern approach to a game steeped in history. Yet, it is also a reminder that every innovation comes with its own set of challenges and controversies, inviting spirited debates among fans, pundits, and players alike.

In the run-up to the Championships, every news cycle, every interview, and every match becomes a part of a larger story. The narratives emerging from the recent season are already setting the stage for what promises to be an unforgettable edition of Wimbledon. There's talk of emerging rivalries that could define careers, of unexpected underdogs ready to upset the established order, and of heart-stopping matches that will undoubtedly become part of tennis folklore.

The anticipation is not limited to the players and the media—fans, too, are gearing up for the spectacle. From the excitement of securing tickets to the palpable buzz on social media, it's clear that Wimbledon 2025 is more than just an event on the calendar; it's a cultural phenomenon that unites people from all walks of life. Whether you're a lifelong devotee or a newcomer to the game, the allure of those hallowed grass courts is irresistible.

Embracing the Future Without Forgetting the Past

In many ways, the story of Wimbledon is a microcosm of the journey we all take through life—a constant balancing act between holding on to cherished traditions and embracing the winds of change. The move towards a fully electronic line-calling system is just one chapter in this ongoing saga. While it may mark the end of an era for some, it also opens up exciting new possibilities for the sport. It's a reminder that while technology can enhance our experience of the game, the real magic lies in the human spirit—the passion, determination, and sheer joy that tennis inspires.

As we prepare to witness Wimbledon 2025, there's an undeniable sense that we are on the cusp of something truly special. The Championships have always been a celebration of excellence, and this year promises to be a fitting tribute to the enduring allure of tennis. With every match, every rally, and every triumphant moment, Wimbledon will continue to inspire, challenge, and captivate audiences around the world.

So, here's to Wimbledon—the tournament that has defined generations, weathered the test of time, and continues to evolve while staying true to its core. As we look forward to the 2025 Championships, we do so with excitement, nostalgia, and an unwavering belief in the beauty of the game. Whether you're a seasoned follower of the sport or a curious newcomer, the story of Wimbledon is one that invites us all to share in the thrill of the chase, the joy of victory, and the bittersweet taste of defeat.

A Celebration of Tennis Heritage

In the final analysis, Wimbledon is much more than a tournament. It's a celebration of tennis heritage—a vibrant tapestry woven from countless moments of brilliance, heartbreak, and triumph. Every swing of the racquet is a brushstroke in a painting that spans decades, a painting that continues to evolve with each passing year. The 2025 Championships are poised to add yet another rich layer to this masterpiece, blending tradition with innovation in a way that only Wimbledon can.

As we turn the page on one chapter and eagerly await the next, the anticipation is almost palpable. There's a shared understanding among fans and players alike that Wimbledon is not just about the present moment, but about a legacy that endures through time. It's a legacy that honours the past while boldly stepping into the future—a future where the spirit of the game remains as vibrant as ever, no matter how many new technologies and innovations come into play.

In this foreword, we've journeyed through the rich corridors of Wimbledon's history, celebrated its timeless traditions, and embraced the exciting narratives that are set to unfold in 2025. The story of Wimbledon is one of constant evolution—a story that reflects the very best of what tennis has to offer: passion, precision, and an unyielding commitment to excellence. As the grass prepares to host another chapter in this illustrious saga, we invite you to join us in celebrating not only the triumphs of the past but also the promise of a future that continues to inspire and enthral.

Here's to Wimbledon 2025—a festival of tennis where tradition meets innovation, where every match is a story waiting to be told, and where the enduring allure of the game continues to captivate hearts around the globe. Cheers to the grass, the players, the fans, and to a tournament that remains, above all, a timeless celebration of the sport we all love.

In a world that is ever-changing, Wimbledon stands as a beacon of continuity—a reminder that while trends may come and go, the essence of tennis endures. It is this enduring spirit that makes the Championships so much more than a sporting event; it makes them a cherished tradition, a source of inspiration, and a rallying point for generations of enthusiasts. As we step into the exciting days ahead, let us raise our glasses to the beauty of Wimbledon—a tournament that not only honours its storied past but also boldly embraces the future with open arms.

So, here we are, on the brink of another remarkable edition of Wimbledon, ready to witness history unfold on those immaculate grass courts. Whether you're relishing the nostalgia of past glories or eagerly anticipating the next breakthrough moment, Wimbledon 2025 promises to be a celebration of everything that makes tennis the sport we adore. With every serve, every volley, and every triumphant cheer, we are reminded that the true magic of Wimbledon lies not just in the triumphs and titles, but in the enduring spirit of the game.

Let the countdown to 2025 begin, and let the narratives, debates, and dreams that have defined Wimbledon for over a century continue to inspire us all. Welcome to Wimbledon—a celebration of heritage, a nod to the future, and a timeless love letter to tennis.

The Road to SW19

The journey to Wimbledon 2025 has been nothing short of a rollercoaster ride, a winding path paved with breathtaking highs, unexpected twists and the kind of drama that makes you want to cheer, commiserate, and then cheer some more. As the tennis world buzzes with anticipation, all eyes are now on SW19—the postcode synonymous with tradition, excellence, and the hallowed grounds where legends are born. With each passing match and every stirring comeback, the road to this iconic tournament is being rewritten, one serve at a time.

Over the past season, the narratives emerging from the tour have been as diverse as they have been enthralling. There's been a palpable shift in momentum, with storylines that could easily be mistaken for the plot of a blockbuster film. For months, we have watched as established names battled to retain their crown, while fresh faces stepped onto centre court with an audacity that belied their inexperience. The 2024 season has provided a treasure trove of moments that are set to define Wimbledon 2025, from nail-biting five-set marathons to unexpected upsets that left us all gasping in disbelief.

There is something truly special about watching a returning champion make their way back to the spotlight. These are the players who have tasted success at the All England Club before, whose names are etched into the history books, and who carry with them the weight of both expectation and legacy. Their journeys have been marked by moments of brilliance and bouts of sheer determination, and their presence in the draw is a reminder of the continuity that underpins this great tournament. Yet, it's not just the old guard that has captured our imagination—there is a palpable excitement around the emerging talents who are stepping up to challenge the established order. The fresh burst of energy from these young guns has injected a new dynamic into the competition, and their rapid rise through the rankings is a testament to both their skill and the evolving nature of the sport.

Throughout the 2024 season, every match seemed to add a new brushstroke to an already vivid canvas. There were players who defied the odds, turning potential upsets into statements of intent, and others who weathered storms of doubt to emerge stronger and more resilient. A number of seasoned contenders, whose careers have been defined by consistency and an unyielding competitive spirit, have found themselves navigating a transformed landscape. The season's rollercoaster of form has reshaped the hierarchy of the tour, impacting player rankings and seedings in ways that will undoubtedly influence the draw at Wimbledon 2025. It's a scenario where yesterday's underdogs could be tomorrow's favourites, and where the balance of power can shift with the flip of a racquet.

The impact of the 2024 season on the rankings has been both profound and unpredictable. Early exits from seemingly straightforward matches sent shockwaves through the rankings, while stellar performances in high-pressure moments allowed a few dark horses to leapfrog their more illustrious rivals. This seismic shift in the standings has not only redefined who is considered a serious contender but has also injected an element of unpredictability into the tournament. As seedings are recalibrated and draws are reshuffled, fans are left wondering who will ultimately rise to the occasion on those pristine grass courts at SW19.

It's fascinating to reflect on the sheer variety of narratives that have unfolded over the past year. Consider the story of a player who, after a series of injuries and setbacks, fought back with a vengeance to reclaim their place among the elite. Their journey was one of determination and grit—a true testament to the spirit of tennis. In another corner of the circuit, a young starlet emerged almost overnight, her meteoric rise marked by a series of jaw-dropping performances that left the tennis fraternity in awe. These are not just isolated stories; they are threads woven into the broader tapestry of the sport, each contributing to the colourful mosaic that is the modern game.

For many, the road to SW19 is as much about personal redemption as it is about athletic excellence. The psychological battles that players face, the mental fortitude required to overcome adversity, and the quiet moments of introspection in the dressing room—all of these have played a crucial role in shaping the narratives that now define the tour. Every victory and every defeat has a story behind it, a story that adds depth and complexity to the journey towards Wimbledon 2025. The beauty of it all lies in the fact that no two journeys are alike; each player's path is uniquely their own, replete with challenges, triumphs, and the occasional heartbreak that only makes the eventual success that much sweeter.

There is also a rich vein of tradition that runs deep through the heart of Wimbledon, and it is this tradition that has both challenged and inspired the players. The legacy of those who have trodden these grounds before is a constant presence—a silent mentor urging every serve, every volley, and every match point to be played with passion and respect. As returning champions step onto the court once again, they do so with a sense of duty and pride, knowing that they are not just competing for a title but for a place in history. Their experiences, honed by years of practice and countless matches, serve as a benchmark for excellence, a standard that the emerging talents aspire to meet and surpass.

Yet, the allure of Wimbledon is not confined solely to its storied past. The present is equally compelling, and the future even more so. With innovations in training techniques, sports science, and even the advent of data analytics in match preparation, the modern player is a far cry from the pioneers of the early 20th century. The interplay between raw talent and technological precision has given rise to a new breed of competitor—one who blends the grace of tradition with the cutting-edge methodologies of today's game. The impact of these advancements was made abundantly clear over the 2024 season, where split-second decisions and razor-sharp reflexes often made the difference between victory and defeat. In many ways, the season has been a showcase of how the sport continues to evolve, and it is this evolution that promises to bring an entirely new level of excitement to Wimbledon 2025.

One cannot help but marvel at the juxtaposition of experience and youth that defines the current crop of players. On one hand, there are the seasoned contenders—veterans who have weathered the highs and lows of a long and storied career. Their wealth of experience, honed through years of grueling competition and hard-fought battles, provides them with an invaluable reservoir of tactical wisdom. On the other hand, the emerging talents bring with them an infectious exuberance, a hunger to prove themselves on the world stage. These young players, many of whom have already made headlines with their fearless play, represent the future of tennis. They are the ones who will carry the torch forward, blending modern flair with the timeless elegance that has come to define the sport.

The road to SW19 has also been marked by some unexpected alliances and rivalries that have added a delightful unpredictability to the mix. In recent tournaments, we've seen erstwhile competitors join forces in doubles events, only to return to fierce individual battles in the singles draw. These shifting dynamics have not only captivated audiences but have also underscored the complexity and multifaceted nature of modern tennis. Rivalries that once seemed set in stone have been redrawn, as players adapt their strategies and forge new relationships on and off the court. It is this fluidity, this willingness to evolve and adapt, that has injected fresh energy into the tour and set the stage for an electrifying Wimbledon 2025.

The effects of the 2024 season are particularly evident when it comes to the reshuffling of player rankings and seedings. For many, these developments have been a wake-up call—a reminder that in the world of professional tennis, nothing is guaranteed. The rankings, often viewed as the ultimate arbiter of success, have been upended by moments of brilliance and bouts of inconsistency alike. Established players who were once considered untouchable have found themselves scrambling to defend their positions, while others have surged ahead, buoyed by a series of stunning performances. The resulting reshuffle has not only altered the competitive landscape but has also raised the stakes for Wimbledon 2025. Every match is now laden with extra significance, as players vie for positions that could make or break their tournament ambitions.

The dramatic shifts in the rankings have also had a profound impact on the tournament's seedings. As the draw for Wimbledon 2025 begins to take shape, fans and pundits alike are speculating on the potential matchups and rivalries that could define the tournament. The prospect of seeing established stars face off against the rising sensations is tantalising, promising a blend of experience and innovation that is sure to set pulses racing. For some, the reshuffle has been a blessing—a chance for long-overdue recognition and a platform to demonstrate that, even in the face of adversity, talent and determination can prevail. For others, it has been a stark reminder of the unforgiving nature of the sport, where a single slip-up can send shockwaves through an entire season.

Throughout the season, the evolution in player form has been mirrored by a growing sense of urgency and determination. Every match, whether it ended in triumph or heartbreak, has added another layer to the narrative that now propels us towards Wimbledon 2025. The highs and lows, the victories and the setbacks, all serve as crucial chapters in a story that is still very much in the making. For the returning champions, every tournament is a chance to reaffirm their dominance, to remind the world of the skill and resilience that have defined their careers. For the emerging talents, it is an opportunity to announce their arrival on the big stage—to show that they are ready to compete with the best of the best.

As we stand on the precipice of Wimbledon 2025, the road that has led us here feels both familiar and brand new. It is a road marked by hard-fought battles, unexpected twists, and the kind of raw emotion that only tennis can evoke. The interplay of experience and youthful exuberance, of tradition and innovation, has created a captivating tapestry that promises to make the upcoming Championships one for the history books. There is a sense that every serve, every rally, and every point played over the past season was a rehearsal for the grand spectacle that awaits at SW19.

Looking back on the 2024 season, one can't help but feel a deep sense of gratitude for the myriad moments that have shaped the current state of the game. From the underdog triumphs that sparked wild celebrations to the epic clashes that tested the limits of endurance and skill, each chapter has contributed to a narrative that is as rich as it is unpredictable. And as the tennis world readies itself for the next chapter, the anticipation is not merely about who will lift the trophy—it is about the journey itself, the passion that drives every player, and the unyielding spirit of competition that defines this beautiful game.

There is, of course, an element of inevitability to this grand narrative. The very nature of tennis is such that every season brings with it the promise of reinvention, a chance to start afresh and rewrite the rules. The 2024 season, with all its surprises and seismic shifts, has laid the foundation for an electrifying Wimbledon 2025. It is a reminder that while the past is a cherished part of Wimbledon's legacy, the future is always ripe with possibility. And as the players prepare to take centre court at SW19, they do so with the full knowledge that every stroke, every footstep, and every moment of brilliance is contributing to a story that will be remembered for generations.

In many ways, the road to SW19 is a microcosm of life itself—a journey filled with challenges, triumphs, setbacks, and moments of sheer magic. It is a journey that celebrates the unpredictable nature of sport, where every match is an opportunity to defy expectations and every victory is a testament to hard work and perseverance. And as we edge closer to Wimbledon 2025, the sense of anticipation is almost palpable—a collective excitement that unites fans, players, and enthusiasts alike in a shared passion for the game.

The narratives that have emerged over the past season are as varied as they are inspiring. They tell the story of a sport in flux, one that honours its illustrious past while eagerly embracing the innovations of tomorrow. Whether it is the emotional return of a champion, the meteoric rise of a newcomer, or the strategic recalibrations forced by an ever-changing competitive landscape, the road to SW19 is rich with intrigue and promise. And while the future remains unwritten, one thing is clear: the journey ahead will be as thrilling and unpredictable as the sport itself.

As we look forward to the grand stage of Wimbledon 2025, there is an undeniable sense that this is more than just a tournament—it is a celebration of the journey, a tribute to the countless hours of dedication, and a recognition of the unbreakable spirit that has propelled the sport to its current heights. The road to SW19 is a journey of dreams and determination, a path that has been carved out by every player who has dared to dream big and every fan who has cheered them on through thick and thin.

In the end, the story of the road to SW19 is a story of transformation—a tale of how the challenges and triumphs of the past season have set the stage for a new era in tennis. It is a story that will be told for years to come, a narrative that captures the very essence of what makes Wimbledon such an extraordinary institution. As we count down the days to Wimbledon 2025, we do so with hearts full of hope, eyes set on the future, and an abiding love for the game that continues to inspire us all.

So, here's to the journey that has brought us to this moment—the triumphs, the setbacks, the surprises and the spectacular moments that have defined the road to SW19. It is a journey that reminds us why we watch, why we cheer, and why we believe in the magic of tennis. And as the stage is set for the next chapter in this incredible saga, we can only wait in eager anticipation for the drama, the passion, and the unforgettable moments that lie ahead at Wimbledon 2025.

Setting the Stage

Wimbledon is a living institution—a realm where the echoes of history meet the relentless beat of modern progress—and as we prepare for the 2025 Championships, the air is thick with anticipation and change. The All England Club, the very heart and soul of Wimbledon, is once again poised to astonish us as it skilfully blends time-honoured tradition with the cutting-edge advancements of the modern era. For those of us who have long adored the ritual of crisp white attire, pristine grass courts, and the reassuring murmur of line judges calling out "Out!" or "Good in," the coming transformation is both exhilarating and, for a few, a touch melancholic. After 147 years of human eyes keeping vigil along the baselines, 2025 will mark a monumental shift: Wimbledon is bidding farewell to the era of line judges, ushering in the age of Live Electronic Line Calling.

It's hard to imagine the familiar figures in smart blazers, ever so stoic in their silent duty, suddenly becoming relics of the past. These are the individuals who have been the unsung heroes behind the scenes, whose acute observations and instantaneous calls have long underpinned the integrity of the game. Now, in a move that reverberates far beyond the boundaries of tradition, the All England Club has declared that technology will take centre stage. The Hawk-Eye system, already a stalwart presence on several courts since 2007, is set to become the sole arbiter of line calls across the entire tournament. This isn't merely a technological upgrade—it's a seismic shift in how the sport will be experienced by players, officials, and fans alike.

At its core, this decision is about consistency and precision. With electronic line calling, every call is made with split-second accuracy, leaving little room for human error or the heated debates that sometimes mar the sport. This change has not come lightly. It follows a "significant period of consideration and consultation," as explained by Sally Bolton, the Chief Executive of the All England Club. Extensive testing during last year's Championships convinced the powers that be that the technology is now sufficiently robust to be trusted with one of the game's most critical functions. For those who have clung to the comforting cadence of human judgement, this new era might feel like an unsettling departure from the familiar. Yet, it is also a natural progression—an inevitable convergence of tradition with modern advancements.

To appreciate the magnitude of this change, one must first understand the unique character of the All England Club. Nestled in the leafy embrace of London, the club has been a bastion of tennis heritage since 1877. Its immaculate lawns, storied architecture, and deep-rooted customs have served as the backdrop for some of the most iconic moments in the sport's history. From the days of wooden racquets and all-white ensembles to the dazzling feats of modern champions, Wimbledon has always been more than just a tournament; it is a celebration of tennis in its purest form. And now, as the club steps boldly into the future, it carries with it the responsibility of preserving that legacy even as it embraces the innovations that define our modern age.

The decision to do away with line judges is emblematic of this delicate balance. On one hand, the tournament has long been a custodian of tradition. For generations, the steady presence of human line judges has been woven into the fabric of Wimbledon's identity. Their role, though often understated, was vital: they were the guardians of fairness, the interpreters of split-second moments that could change the course of a match. Yet, as the world of tennis has evolved, so too have the demands of the modern game. With faster play, more intricate strategies, and an ever-increasing reliance on data and technology, the need for precision has never been greater. The move to electronic line calling is, in many respects, a natural evolution—a necessary adaptation that ensures the sport remains as accurate and fair as possible.

This transformation is not occurring in isolation. It comes on the back of a broader shift within professional tennis. The ATP's decision to roll out electronic line calling at all men's tour events from 2025 has set the stage for this change at Wimbledon. No longer is the All England Club willing to cling to tradition merely for nostalgia's sake or to satisfy the expectations of long-time sponsors. Instead, it has chosen to lead by example, demonstrating that even the most storied institutions can adapt and innovate. In doing so, Wimbledon is not only preserving its competitive integrity but also signalling to the rest of the sporting world that technology and tradition can, indeed, coexist.

SETTING THE STAGE

There is a certain poetry in the way the past and the future are colliding at Wimbledon. Picture this: the hushed silence that falls over Centre Court as the final point of a match is played, punctuated by the digital confirmation of a call made in a fraction of a second. It is a moment that is at once familiar and startlingly new—a reminder that while the spirit of the game remains unchanged, its execution has entered a new era. For traditionalists, this shift may evoke a sense of loss, as the human touch that once defined the experience is replaced by the cold precision of computer algorithms. But for many, it represents progress—a step towards a game where every call is as objective as it is instantaneous, where the margin for error is reduced and the integrity of the competition is further safeguarded.

The implications of this change extend far beyond the visual spectacle of a digital display. With the human eye removed from the equation, one of the traditional pathways into the world of tennis officiating comes to an abrupt end. For decades, aspiring umpires have dreamt of donning the smart blazer and stepping up to the baseline, contributing in a quiet yet essential way to the flow of the game. Now, as artificial intelligence continues to evolve and assert its dominance, that dream may soon belong only to the annals of tennis history. Yet, even as this chapter closes, the spirit of those dedicated officials is honoured in the meticulous care with which the transition has been managed. Their years of service and commitment to the game are acknowledged with gratitude, even as the tournament prepares to chart a bold new course.

One of the most fascinating aspects of this transformation is how it encapsulates the broader cultural shift towards technology in sport. We live in an era where data, analytics, and artificial intelligence have permeated nearly every facet of our lives. From the instantaneous feedback provided by smartwatches to the intricate algorithms that predict everything from weather patterns to financial markets, technology is reshaping our world. Tennis, with its reliance on split-second decisions and razor-sharp reflexes, is a natural playground for such innovations. The move towards electronic line calling at Wimbledon is not an isolated experiment—it is part of a global trend in sports, where technology is increasingly seen as the key to unlocking new levels of performance and fairness.

Consider, for instance, the transformative impact of VAR in football. Although its implementation has sparked heated debates and sometimes polarised opinions among fans, the underlying principle remains the same: technology is being deployed to reduce human error and ensure that the spirit of fair play is upheld. In a similar vein, the adoption of the Hawk-Eye system at Wimbledon promises to bring about a level of consistency that has long been sought after in tennis. No longer will fans, commentators, or players be left wondering if a call was influenced by a momentary lapse in human concentration. Instead, every decision will be underpinned by the unwavering logic of sophisticated software, designed to process visual data with unerring accuracy.

Of course, the transition is not without its detractors. There are those who argue that the human element—the intuition, the experience, and even the occasional controversial call—adds a layer of unpredictability and character to the sport. They reminisce fondly about the days when a well-timed "Out!" from a seasoned line judge could become an integral part of the match's narrative. For these traditionalists, the shift to electronic line calling feels like a loss of a cherished ritual, a piece of the magic that makes Wimbledon unique. Yet, even as they grieve the fading presence of the familiar, there is a grudging acceptance that progress is inevitable. After all, no institution, no matter how steeped in history, is immune to the march of time and the imperatives of modernity.

In the grand tapestry of Wimbledon's illustrious history, the coming changes are but one thread—a bold and vibrant one that speaks to the tournament's ongoing evolution. The move to ditch line judges is not a rejection of tradition; rather, it is an acknowledgement that the spirit of Wimbledon can endure and thrive even as the mechanisms that support it evolve. It is a celebration of innovation that does not erase the past, but builds upon it, ensuring that the essence of the game remains untarnished even as its tools become more advanced.

Beyond the technical adjustments, there are other significant changes on the horizon for Wimbledon 2025. The tournament organisers have announced a reshuffling of the schedule that reflects a desire to modernise the viewing experience and accommodate a global audience. From next year, the singles finals on the final weekend will be moved from their traditional 2pm slots to a later 4pm start, while the men's and women's doubles finals will now kick off at 1pm. These adjustments, though seemingly minor in comparison to the switch in officiating, are part and parcel of Wimbledon's broader strategy to balance its storied past with the demands of today's media and broadcast landscape. The changes are designed to capture prime-time audiences, both in the UK and around the world, ensuring that the magic of Wimbledon reaches as many fans as possible.

This reorganisation of the schedule is a further testament to Wimbledon's willingness to innovate without compromising its core values. The tournament has always been a pioneer, not just in the realm of tennis but in the wider sphere of sports. Its ability to adapt to changing times while preserving its unique traditions is a quality that has endeared it to millions across the globe. In a world where the pace of change can sometimes feel overwhelming, Wimbledon stands as a reassuring reminder that progress and heritage can walk hand in hand. The new schedule, much like the new technology, is a carefully considered response to the evolving needs of a diverse and dynamic audience. It is an invitation to a new generation of fans, offering them a fresh perspective on a tournament that has captivated hearts for over a century.

Of course, the shift to electronic line calling also raises important questions about the future of officiating in tennis. With the removal of the human line judge, one wonders what other traditional roles might be subject to technological takeover in the years to come. It is a topic that has sparked lively debate among players, officials, and fans alike. While some worry about the potential loss of the personal touch that has long defined Wimbledon, others are excited by the prospect of a more streamlined, efficient, and objective system. In many ways, this debate mirrors broader discussions about technology's role in society—a dialogue about what we stand to gain from innovation, and what we might lose along the way.

Yet, if one thing is certain, it is that the All England Club has approached this monumental change with a deep sense of responsibility. Every decision has been taken with the utmost care, ensuring that the tournament's integrity remains intact even as its format is transformed. Sally Bolton's measured words remind us that this change is not a whim, but the result of rigorous testing, extensive consultation, and an unwavering commitment to excellence. The club's decision is rooted in the desire to offer players a consistent playing environment, one that aligns with the conditions they encounter at other major tournaments across the globe. In this light, the move is less about abandoning tradition and more about ensuring that Wimbledon continues to deliver the highest standards of competitive fairness and precision.

There is an undeniable charm in the way Wimbledon has always managed to be both a bastion of tradition and a beacon of innovation. The tournament's evolution over the years is a reflection of its ability to adapt while staying true to its core ethos—a balance that is now being tested like never before. The forthcoming technological overhaul, while stirring mixed emotions among the purists, is also a bold affirmation of Wimbledon's commitment to progress. It is a declaration that, in the face of inevitable change, the spirit of the game remains inviolable. Every digital call made by the Hawk-Eye system is a testament to the relentless march of technology, yet it also honours the legacy of every match, every player, and every moment that has made Wimbledon the hallowed ground it is today.

As we stand on the threshold of this new chapter, it is impossible not to feel a sense of wonder at the transformative power of innovation. The All England Club, with its deep reverence for history and its visionary embrace of modernity, is charting a course that will undoubtedly leave an indelible mark on the future of tennis. The coming changes are not merely adjustments to the rulebook—they are a reimagining of what Wimbledon can be, a fusion of the past and the present that promises to captivate audiences for generations to come.

For many fans, the idea of a Wimbledon without line judges is bittersweet. It conjures memories of legendary matches punctuated by the distinctive calls of officiating legends and the palpable tension of disputed points. Yet, it also heralds a future where every call is made with impeccable precision—a future where the spirit of the game is preserved through the impartial lens of technology. As we watch the digital displays light up Centre Court and listen to the soft hum of cameras capturing every angle, we are reminded that the essence of tennis is not diminished by the tools we use, but rather, it is enriched by our ability to innovate and adapt.

In the end, the decision to embrace Live Electronic Line Calling is a reflection of Wimbledon's enduring commitment to excellence. It is a move that honours the past by learning from it, while boldly stepping into the future with confidence and clarity. The legacy of the tournament is not defined solely by the rituals and routines of yesteryear, but by its willingness to evolve and meet the challenges of tomorrow head-on. With every serve, every volley, and every electrifying rally, Wimbledon continues to write its storied history—a history that is now being enhanced by the brilliance of modern technology.

As the countdown to the 2025 Championships begins, the excitement surrounding these changes is palpable. The All England Club is not just hosting a tournament; it is orchestrating a celebration of progress, a fusion of tradition and innovation that will captivate the hearts and minds of tennis fans around the world. The forthcoming era of electronic line calling is set to redefine the game, delivering a level of consistency and accuracy that will undoubtedly set new benchmarks for excellence. And while the familiar faces of the line judges may soon fade into the annals of history, their legacy will live on in the stories of matches won, records shattered, and the unwavering spirit of Wimbledon.

In this brave new world, where algorithms and cameras replace the human eye, the true magic of Wimbledon will continue to shine through. It is the passion of the players, the fervour of the fans, and the deep-rooted traditions of the All England Club that have always made Wimbledon more than just a tennis tournament. They have made it a celebration of life, a gathering of hearts united by the love of the game. And as we step into this era of digital precision, we do so with the understanding that while the instruments of our craft may change, the soul of Wimbledon remains as vibrant and enduring as ever.

So, as we set the stage for Wimbledon 2025, let us embrace the spirit of innovation without losing sight of the traditions that have made this tournament a beacon of tennis excellence. Let us celebrate the remarkable journey that has brought us here—a journey marked by both the timeless elegance of yesteryear and the dynamic promise of tomorrow. In every match that unfolds on those hallowed grass courts, in every decision rendered by the unblinking gaze of technology, we will witness a testament to the enduring power of progress and the unwavering commitment to fair play.

The stage is set, the players are ready, and the world watches in anticipation. Wimbledon, with its rich heritage and its bold leap into the future, stands as a shining example of how we can honour our past while boldly embracing the possibilities of tomorrow. As the digital era dawns on this venerable institution, the promise of a new chapter is written in every pixel and every line call—a promise that the spirit of tennis will continue to inspire, innovate, and unite us all.

And so, as we bid farewell to the era of the human line judge and welcome the precision of Live Electronic Line Calling, we do so with both a sense of nostalgia and a spirited optimism for what lies ahead. The transformation at Wimbledon is more than a mere change in officiating; it is a profound reimagining of how tradition and technology can coexist, creating an experience that is as captivating as it is fair. With every match that unfolds, we are reminded that progress does not mean the loss of our cherished heritage—it means the evolution of it, enhanced by the brilliance of modern innovation.

In the final analysis, the decision to remove line judges and fully embrace technology is emblematic of Wimbledon's enduring commitment to remain at the forefront of tennis. It is a change that honours the past while ensuring that the future is even brighter, more precise, and filled with endless possibilities. As we stand on the precipice of this new era, we celebrate not just the advancements in technology, but the spirit of adaptation that has always defined this great tournament. The All England Club, with its seamless blend of tradition and modernity, continues to inspire us all to look forward with hope and excitement, knowing that the heart of Wimbledon beats as strongly as ever.

In welcoming this change, we are also acknowledging that every innovation is a step towards creating a more perfect game—one where the margin for error is narrowed and the beauty of tennis is captured in every measured, precise moment. The countdown to Wimbledon 2025 is more than a mere marking of time; it is a celebration of evolution, a tribute to the relentless pursuit of excellence that has defined the sport for generations.

As we take our seats in the stands and prepare to witness history in the making, we do so with the firm belief that while the tools may change, the essence of Wimbledon remains constant—a constant reminder of why we love tennis, why we celebrate its heroes, and why we remain forever enchanted by the magic of the game.

Here's to Wimbledon 2025—a tournament where tradition meets technology, where the past is honoured even as the future unfolds in dazzling digital clarity. The stage is set, the digital whistle has blown, and the next chapter in this grand saga is about to begin.

WEEK ONE

From Monday 30 June through Sunday 6 July, the tournament kicks off with a packed schedule of action. It all begins with the Gentlemen's and Ladies' Singles First Round on Monday and Tuesday. By Wednesday and Thursday, the singles move into the Second Round, while the Doubles competitions for both gentlemen and ladies start their First Round.

Day	Schedule
Mon 30 June	Gentlemen's and Ladies' Singles First Round
Tue 1 July	Gentlemen's and Ladies' Singles First Round
Wed 2 July	Gentlemen's and Ladies' Singles Second Round Gentlemen's & Ladies' Doubles First Round
Thu 3 July	Gentlemen's and Ladies' Singles Second Round Gentlemen's & Ladies' Doubles First Round
Fri 4 July	Gentlemen's and Ladies' Singles Third Round Gentlemen's & Ladies' Doubles Second Round Mixed Doubles First Round
Sat 5 July	Gentlemen's and Ladies' Singles Third Round Gentlemen's & Ladies' Doubles Second Round Mixed Doubles First Round Boys' and Girls' Singles First Round (18&U)
Sun 6 July	Gentlemen's and Ladies' Singles Fourth Round Gentlemen's & Ladies' Doubles Third Round Mixed Doubles Second Round Boys' and Girls' Singles First Round (18&U)

On Friday, the Singles enter the Third Round, the Doubles advance to the Second Round, and the Mixed Doubles make their debut in the First Round. Saturday mirrors Friday's schedule with additional Mixed Doubles play and introduces the Boys' and Girls' Singles First Round for players under 18. The week culminates on Sunday with the

Singles reaching the Fourth Round, the Doubles moving into the Third Round, the Mixed Doubles progressing to the Second Round, and the Youth Singles continuing.

WEEK TWO

Mon 7 July	Gentlemen's and Ladies' Singles Fourth Round Gentlemen's & Ladies' Doubles Third Round Mixed Doubles Quarter-finals Girls' Singles Second Round (18&U) Boys' Doubles First Round (18&U)
Tue 8 July	Gentlemen's and Ladies' Singles Quarter-finals Gentlemen's & Ladies' Doubles Quarter-finals Mixed Doubles Semi-finals Gentlemen's and Ladies' Wheelchair Singles First Round Boys' Singles Second Round (18&U) Girls' Doubles First Round (18&U) Invitation Doubles (Ladies' Doubles, Gentlemen's Doubles, Mixed Doubles)
Wed 9 July	Gentlemen's and Ladies' Singles Quarter-finals Gentlemen's & Ladies' Doubles Quarter-finals Quad Wheelchair Singles Quarter-finals Gentlemen's and Ladies' Wheelchair Doubles Quarter-finals Boys' & Girls' Singles Third Round (18&U) Boys' & Girls' Doubles Second Round (18&U) Invitation Doubles (Ladies' Doubles, Gentlemen's Doubles, Mixed Doubles)
Thu 10 July	Ladies' Singles Semi-finals Gentlemen's Doubles Semi-finals Mixed Doubles Final Gentlemen's and Ladies' Wheelchair Singles Quarter-finals Gentlemen's, Ladies' & Quad Wheelchair Doubles Semi-finals Boys' & Girls' Singles Quarter-finals (18&U) Boys' & Girls' Doubles Quarter-finals (18&U) Boys' and Girls' 14&U Singles Invitation Doubles (Ladies' Doubles, Gentlemen's Doubles, Mixed Doubles)
Fri 11 July	Gentlemen's Singles Semi-finals Ladies' Doubles Semi-finals Gentlemen's, Ladies' & Quad Wheelchair Singles Semi-finals Boys' & Girls' Singles Semi-finals (18&U) Boys' & Girls' Doubles Semi-finals (18&U) Boys' and Girls' 14&U Singles Invitation Doubles (Ladies' Doubles, Gentlemen's Doubles, Mixed Doubles)
Sat 12 July	Gentlemen's Doubles Final Ladies' Singles Final Ladies' Wheelchair Singles Final Gentlemen's & Quad Wheelchair Doubles Final Girls' Singles Final (18&U) Girls' Doubles Final (18&U) Boys' Doubles Final (18&U) Boys' and Girls' 14&U Singles Semi-finals Invitation Doubles (Ladies' Doubles, Gentlemen's Doubles, Mixed Doubles)
Sun 13 July	Ladies' Doubles Final Gentlemen's Singles Final Gentlemen's & Quad Wheelchair Singles Finals Ladies' Wheelchair Doubles Final Boys' Singles Final (18&U) Boys' & Girls' 14&U Singles Finals Invitation Doubles (Ladies' Doubles, Gentlemen's Doubles, Mixed Doubles)

THE TOURNAMENT TIME TABLE: WEEKS ONE & TWO

From Monday 7 July through Sunday 13 July, the Wimbledon courts come alive with a whirlwind of drama, passion, and breakthrough moments that promise to leave fans breathless. The week kicks off on Monday 7 July with a thrilling start as both the Gentlemen's and Ladies' Singles enter their Fourth Round. The tension is palpable as top seeds and dark horses alike battle it out for a coveted spot in the later stages. At the same time, the Doubles field heats up with the Gentlemen's and Ladies' teams competing in the Third Round, setting the stage for dynamic displays of teamwork and strategy. The Mixed Doubles action reaches a critical point with the Quarter-finals underway, where unexpected twists could tip the balance in favour of the boldest pairs. In the junior arena, excitement builds with the Girls' Singles for under-18 players stepping into the Second Round, while the Boys' Doubles kick off with their very First Round—a day that heralds the emergence of tomorrow's stars.

Tuesday 8 July sees the intensity ramp up even further. The Singles draw shifts into the Quarter-finals, with both Gentlemen's and Ladies' competitions promising nail-biting encounters as the remaining players vie for a place among the elite. The Doubles battles intensify too, as teams in both the Gentlemen's and Ladies' events clash in their own Quarter-finals, each point fought with the precision of chess masters. Meanwhile, the Mixed Doubles move into the Semi-finals, where every match point is a potential turning point. On a different front, the Wheelchair Singles make their debut for the day with both the Gentlemen's and Ladies' competitions starting their First Round, adding another layer of excitement to the week. The under-18 events also continue as the Boys' Singles enter their Second Round and the Girls' Doubles commence their First Round, while the Invitation Doubles events—involving Ladies', Gentlemen's, and Mixed Doubles—offer a delightful showcase of seasoned talent and exhibition brilliance.

The midweek action on Wednesday 9 July is a festival of tennis in all its diversity. The Singles Quarter-finals for both Gentlemen and Ladies continue to captivate audiences with matches that combine raw athleticism and razor-sharp tactics. In parallel, the Doubles competitions in both the Gentlemen's and Ladies' draws remain fiercely contested in their Quarter-finals, with every team leaving no stone unturned. The Quad Wheelchair Singles and the Wheelchair Doubles for both Gentlemen and Ladies also enter their Quarter-finals, highlighting the incredible skill and determination of these outstanding athletes. Junior tennis is in full swing too, with both Boys' and Girls' Singles reaching the Third Round and their Doubles events advancing to the Second Round in the under-18 category. The Invitation

Doubles, a fan-favourite event showcasing a blend of established stars and emerging talent, adds its own unique flavour to this action-packed day.

Thursday 10 July marks a pivotal turning point in the tournament as the stakes soar to new heights. The Ladies' Singles Semi-finals deliver a dramatic mix of power, precision, and mental fortitude, with each player determined to secure a place in the final. On the men's side, the Doubles draw heats up as teams clash in the Semi-finals, setting the stage for spectacular partnerships to emerge. The Mixed Doubles final takes centre stage, promising an edge-of-your-seat spectacle that encapsulates the spirit of Wimbledon's dynamic format. The Wheelchair Singles—both Gentlemen's and Ladies'—continue their battle in the Quarter-finals, while the Doubles events across the Gentlemen's, Ladies', and Quad Wheelchair categories progress into the Semi-finals, each match a testament to teamwork and adaptability. Junior competition also reaches a critical juncture: both the Boys' and Girls' Singles in the under-18 bracket advance to the Quarter-finals, and their Doubles events follow suit. Adding to the excitement, the Boys' and Girls' Singles for the 14-and-under category start their battles, while the Invitation Doubles continue to enthral audiences with their signature blend of skill and entertainment.

Friday 11 July ramps up the drama as the tournament enters its final stretch before the climactic weekend. The Gentlemen's Singles Semi-finals set the tone for what promises to be an epic showdown, with players pushing themselves to the very limit in a bid to secure a spot in the final. In the Doubles arena, the Ladies' Doubles Semi-finals are a masterclass in coordination and power, while the Wheelchair Singles—across Gentlemen's, Ladies', and Quad categories—advance to their own Semi-finals, each match a showcase of resilience and precision. The under-18 competition intensifies as both the Singles and Doubles events for Boys and Girls reach the Semi-finals, with young stars displaying nerves of steel and flair beyond their years. The Boys' and Girls' 14-and-under Singles continue to test the mettle of the youngest competitors, and the Invitation Doubles remain a delightful, high-spirited affair that bridges generations with its celebratory atmosphere.

Saturday 12 July is a day when dreams are realised and the very best of Wimbledon come to the fore. The Gentlemen's Doubles Final promises fireworks as teams battle for supremacy on the hallowed grass, while the Ladies' Singles Final is set to be an emotional rollercoaster where every stroke counts. In the Wheelchair competitions, the Ladies' Singles Final and the Gentlemen's & Quad Wheelchair Doubles Final are expected to deliver inspirational moments that underscore the sheer determination of these incredible athletes. The junior tournaments continue to captivate as the Girls' Singles Final and Girls' Doubles Final in the under-18 category, along with the Boys' Doubles Final, add their own chapters to the rich legacy of youth tennis at Wimbledon. The Boys' and Girls' 14-and-under Singles Semi-finals offer one last glimpse of emerging talent before the finals, and the Invitation Doubles, as always, round off the day with a celebration of tennis artistry and camaraderie.

The grand finale on Sunday 13 July brings the week's excitement to a breathtaking climax. The Ladies' Doubles Final promises to be a showcase of refined skill and partnership, while the Gentlemen's Singles Final is the pinnacle of the tournament—a high-stakes battle where every point is a potential piece of history. In a dual spectacle of determination and brilliance, the Gentlemen's & Quad Wheelchair Singles Finals take centre stage, illustrating the evolution and inclusivity of modern tennis. The Ladies' Wheelchair Doubles Final adds another layer of intensity and inspiration to the day, ensuring that every facet of the game is celebrated. The under-18 excitement continues as the Boys' Singles Final in this category unfolds, and the Boys' & Girls' 14-and-under Singles Finals deliver a fitting tribute to the future of the sport. Rounding off the day, the Invitation Doubles—featuring Ladies', Gentlemen's, and Mixed Doubles—offer a final burst of celebratory tennis, uniting past and present in a dazzling display of skill, tradition, and unbridled passion.

Throughout this exhilarating week, every match, every set, and every moment contributes to a narrative of passion, perseverance, and the unyielding spirit of competition that defines Wimbledon. From the early battles on Monday to the crowning moments on Sunday, the tournament encapsulates the magic of tennis—a magic that is built on the promise of new beginnings, the thrill of unexpected twists, and the timeless celebration of excellence on grass. Fans, players, and coaches alike are united in their anticipation for each serve, every volley, and the historic moments that are destined to be etched into the annals of this great sporting tradition.

The Early Rounds

The early rounds have burst onto the scene with all the excitement and unpredictability that Wimbledon fans have come to expect. From the moment the players stepped onto the hallowed grass, the air was buzzing with anticipation. Matches unfolded with moments of brilliance, unexpected upsets, and standout performances that have already ignited countless conversations in locker rooms and living rooms alike. Established names have been challenged by hungry newcomers, and the intensity of every rally has been a vivid reminder that nothing is set in stone in this grand tournament.

There have been several matches that could easily be described as mini epics. Picture a veteran stalwart, known for his unyielding determination, being pushed to his physical and mental limits by a young gun whose aggressive serve-and-volley tactics left the crowd in rapturous disbelief. In one particularly memorable five-set thriller, both players dug deep into their reservoirs of stamina and skill, exchanging momentum like seasoned chess grandmasters. These marathon encounters aren't just tests of physical endurance; they're narratives of perseverance and the raw emotional energy that only Wimbledon can offer.

Home support has been a major talking point in these early stages. British players, bolstered by passionate crowds, have been drawing cheers and chants that echo around Centre Court and beyond. The atmosphere has been electric—every point contested not only for pride and ranking but also for the undying support of fans who have come out in droves. Their performances have been a delightful mix of grit, flashes of brilliance, and, on occasion, the occasional misstep that reminds us all of the unforgiving nature of competitive tennis. The

THE EARLY ROUNDS

local heroes have not only provided moments of joy but also set the stage for emerging storylines that hint at a promising future for British tennis.

The early rounds have also been a showcase for emerging storylines. The grass has borne witness to dramatic five-set battles where momentum swung like a pendulum. These encounters have not only thrilled fans but also signalled that underdogs have every chance to upset the established order. Every unexpected victory has added a fresh layer to the tournament's rich narrative, challenging preconceptions and inviting debate about which rising star might just become the next Wimbledon hero. Such matches, replete with nail-biting finishes and dramatic shifts in fortune, remind us why the early rounds are often the most unpredictable and exhilarating part of the Championships.

Second Week Showdowns

As the tournament shifts into its second week, the stakes have soared to even greater heights. The quarter-finals and semi-finals have emerged as the definitive battlegrounds where every match carries the weight of history. Here, the tension is palpable as each serve and return becomes a pivotal turning point that could make or break a player's campaign. These key matches are not just about progressing through the draw; they are the crucible in which rivalries are both rekindled and newly forged.

The quarter-final clashes have been a masterclass in competitive spirit. Players are now acutely aware that every point is critical, and the pressure has transformed each match into a fiercely contested battle. One can hardly overlook the strategic brilliance on display as athletes recalibrate their game plans on the fly, determined to seize any opportunity that presents itself. In these encounters, a single unforced error can dramatically alter the complexion of a match, and every game has the potential to turn into a turning point that propels a player closer to the final.

As the dust settles on the quarter-finals, the semi-finals have taken the drama up several notches. It is in these later stages that long-standing rivalries have been reignited, drawing on memories of past battles that have defined careers. At the same time, fresh rivalries are emerging—rivalries built on the sparks that fly during intense, all-or-nothing moments on the court. The semi-final matches have been a blend of high-octane energy, meticulous strategy, and moments of pure, unadulterated brilliance. Every decisive shot and well-fought rally has added a new chapter to the ongoing saga of this year's Championships.

SECOND WEEK SHOWDOWNS

In the midst of this high drama, the emotional undercurrents of the tournament have become more pronounced. Several players, who have graced the tour for many years, have experienced emotional farewells as their journeys draw to a close. These farewells are not marked by bitterness but by a sense of gratitude and nostalgia, as fans and fellow competitors alike salute careers that have contributed so richly to the sport's heritage. Their departures are poignant reminders of the fleeting nature of athletic careers and the constant renewal that keeps Wimbledon vibrant year after year.

The second week has also proved to be a fertile ground for emerging talent. Several underdogs, having impressed in the early rounds, are now stepping up to challenge the established elite. Their performances have been characterised by a refreshing audacity and flair—attributes that hint at a promising future in the sport. These new contenders are not just fighting for a place in the next round; they are making statements about the next generation of tennis. Every decisive point they win adds another brushstroke to the canvas of a tournament that is as much about legacy as it is about immediate glory.

There is something particularly compelling about the way strategy, endurance, and sheer willpower converge in these second-week showdowns. Players are not merely contending with each other but with the relentless pressure of high expectations. The marathon matches, often lasting well into the evening, are as much tests of mental fortitude as they are of physical capability. It is in these moments of exhaustion and exhilaration that the true character of a player is revealed. The way an athlete recovers from a break down or rallies from a deficit often speaks louder than any pre-tournament predictions, and it is these moments that will be remembered long after the final whistle.

All of these elements combine to set the stage for an electrifying conclusion to the Championships. The early rounds have been a prelude filled with surprises, while the second week of showdowns has delivered the kind of high-stakes drama that defines the essence of Wimbledon. From the passionate support for British players to the emergence of new rivalries and the emotional farewells of long-serving stalwarts, every element of the tournament contributes to a rich tapestry of competition and camaraderie.

In the final analysis, the journey from the early rounds to the second week of showdowns encapsulates the beauty of Wimbledon. It is a journey marked by moments of triumph and despair, of tactical brilliance and raw, unfiltered emotion. As the tournament moves inexorably towards its climax, fans are left with a sense of anticipation that only a competition of this calibre can inspire. Every match, every set, and every point played is a stepping stone on the road to glory, and each narrative thread adds depth to an already compelling story.

These chapters in the tournament not only highlight the sheer unpredictability of tennis but also celebrate the human spirit—the passion, the perseverance, and the occasional heartbreak that remind us why we love the game. With the quarter-finals and semi-finals drawing ever closer, the stage is set for a finale that promises to be as dramatic and unforgettable as the journey that led us here.

Novak Djokovic Carlos Alcaraz Iga Swiatek Ons Jabeur

The Women's Championship

The story of this year's Women's Championship is one of passion, resilience, and transformation—a saga that has captivated fans from the first serve to the final rally. At the heart of this narrative stands the 2024 champion, Barbora Krejčíková, whose remarkable performance has not only reaffirmed her status among the elite but has also sparked a fresh wave of optimism for the future of women's tennis. As we delve into an in-depth analysis of the women's final and trace the champion's journey through the tournament, we uncover a rich tapestry of memorable moments, tactical masterstrokes, and broader implications for the sport that promise to shape its landscape for years to come.

Barbora Krejčíková's triumph in 2024 is a story of grit and brilliance. Known for her elegant style on court and her uncanny ability to turn defence into offence, Krejčíková has long been admired for her versatility and tactical nous. Her win was never in doubt from the moment she first stepped onto the grass, but it was the manner in which she dominated the draw that truly set her apart. Many commentators and aficionados alike were struck by her composure under pressure—a quality that shone brightest during the final, where every point was contested with razor-sharp precision. As she weaved through her opponents' defences, Krejčíková displayed a blend of athleticism and artistry that reminded us all why tennis is as much about finesse as it is about physicality.

The final itself was a spectacle of determination and tactical brilliance. It was a contest where every serve, every volley, and every baseline rally carried the weight of expectation. From the outset, Krejčíková's opponent challenged her in ways that demanded both strategic adjustments and emotional fortitude. The match unfolded like a finely crafted drama, with twists that left the crowd gasping and then applauding in equal measure. At key junctures, when the scoreline teetered on a knife's edge, it was Krejčíková's ability to remain calm that made all the difference. She responded to each surge in momentum with counterattacks that were as unexpected as they were effective, often turning the tables on her rival with a combination of well-placed drop shots and powerful groundstrokes.

Beyond the immediate tactical battles, the final held broader implications for the world of women's tennis. For decades, the sport has been defined by a delicate balance between tradition and the relentless drive for innovation. Krejčíková's performance, with its blend of classical technique and modern athleticism, symbolised this synthesis perfectly. Her win was not just a personal triumph but a moment of affirmation for a generation of players who are reshaping the narrative of women's tennis. In an era where every match is dissected down to the minutest detail on social media and in analysis shows across the globe, her ability to maintain grace under pressure has sent a resounding message about the enduring value of skill, experience, and mental toughness.

The championship final also highlighted the evolving nature of match strategy in the women's game. Spectators witnessed a battle of wits, where tactics were as crucial as physical prowess. Krejčíková's careful selection of shots—her decision to use angles to pull her opponent off the court, her willingness to mix in delicate slices with powerful strokes—demonstrated a nuanced understanding of her own strengths and her rival's weaknesses. Analysts have since pointed out that this match could well serve as a blueprint for future finals, where the balance of aggression and patience will be key. The impact of such a tactical approach extends beyond the confines of one match; it hints at a broader shift in the sport, where versatility and adaptability are becoming as prized as raw power.

Yet, it is perhaps the champion's journey through the tournament that captures the imagination most vividly. From the opening round, Krejčíková's path was marked by moments that were equal parts inspiring and nerve-wracking. Her early matches provided glimpses of a player who was not only physically prepared but also mentally resolute. There were instances where she found herself in seemingly precarious situations—fighting back from deficits, or being forced into marathon rallies that tested every fibre of her determination. In these matches, the evolution of her game was evident: every long rally and every crucial breakpoint served as a stepping stone that refined her strategy and boosted her confidence.

Throughout the tournament, one of the most striking features of her campaign was her unwavering commitment to maintaining a positive

THE WOMEN'S CHAMPIONSHIP

mindset. In interviews off the court, Krejčíková spoke candidly about the challenges of competing at such a high level, particularly in an environment where every point is scrutinised by millions. Her words resonated with fans who have long admired her forthright honesty and humble approach. It wasn't just about winning the match—it was about embracing the journey, learning from every setback, and emerging stronger each time. This journey was punctuated by a series of memorable matches that not only tested her physical limits but also showcased her ability to adapt under pressure. Whether it was a sudden downpour during an outdoor match that altered the playing conditions or a pivotal moment when she broke her opponent's momentum with a perfectly executed lob, each instance added another rich layer to her championship narrative.

Moreover, her journey was a microcosm of the broader challenges and triumphs faced by women's tennis today. In recent years, the sport has seen an influx of young talent eager to make their mark, and Krejčíková's campaign served as a masterclass in how experience can be the ultimate differentiator. While new faces dazzled with raw power and fearless aggression, it was Krejčíková's measured, almost poetic approach to the game that ultimately won the day. Her journey from the early rounds to the final was punctuated by moments of sheer brilliance, and each victory reinforced the notion that consistency, perseverance, and a deep understanding of the game are indispensable assets. Her steady progression through the tournament provided a blueprint for aspiring players, highlighting that success is not an overnight phenomenon but the culmination of hard work, strategy, and an indomitable spirit.

Beyond her individual achievements, the impact of Krejčíková's championship win on the women's tennis landscape is profound. The win is set to reverberate across the sport, influencing everything from training methodologies to tactical approaches. Coaches and analysts are already lauding the final as a turning point—one that could redefine how future champions are nurtured and how matches are strategised at the highest level. The tournament has provided a powerful narrative for the potential of modern women's tennis: a sport that honours its traditions while continuously pushing the boundaries of what is possible.

The implications of her victory extend to the commercial and cultural dimensions of the sport as well. With a global audience watching, Krejčíková's performance has the power to inspire a new generation of players, especially in regions where women's tennis has yet to receive its full due recognition. Her triumph is being celebrated not only as a personal achievement but as a milestone that could galvanise support for further investment in the women's game. From grassroots programmes to elite training academies, there is a growing realisation that the future of tennis depends on nurturing talent and providing opportunities for female athletes to excel on the world stage.

In the wake of her championship, conversations among fans, commentators, and former players have taken on an almost celebratory tone. There is a shared sense of optimism that the strategic innovations and relentless drive displayed by Krejčíková will usher in a new era for women's tennis—one characterised by greater parity, heightened competition, and a renewed focus on technical brilliance. Her win has opened up discussions about the evolving dynamics between experience and youth, and how these elements can coexist to produce truly captivating contests. Moreover, her success is prompting a re-examination of long-held beliefs about the limits of athletic endurance and the power of mental strength—a discussion that is likely to influence coaching strategies and player development for years to come.

As the dust settles on this year's Women's Championship, it becomes clear that Barbora Krejčíková's triumph is more than just a title win—it is a catalyst for change. It is a statement that the sport is evolving, and that the future of women's tennis will be defined by a blend of tactical ingenuity, relentless determination, and an unwavering commitment to excellence. The championship final, with its twists, turns, and breathtaking moments, will undoubtedly be remembered as one of the most riveting contests in recent memory. And as we look ahead, the impact of this match will continue to be felt—not just in the record books, but in the very fabric of the sport.

The championship has also ignited a renewed debate about the state of women's tennis, prompting discussions about how the game can continue to grow and adapt in a rapidly changing sporting environment. With advances in technology, analytics, and sports science, the tools available to players today are more sophisticated than ever before. Krejčíková's journey through the tournament, marked by her innovative shot selection and strategic adaptability, serves as a vivid illustration of how modern techniques can be harmoniously integrated with traditional skill. This synthesis of old and new is already beginning to influence training routines and match preparations, as coaches look to harness the power of data-driven insights to complement the intuitive knowledge that comes with years on the tour.

There is also an important cultural shift underway. For many years, women's tennis has fought for equal recognition and resources, and champions like Krejčíková are at the forefront of this movement. Her success is not only a triumph for her personally but also a vindication for the countless female athletes who have battled against the odds to secure their place on the international stage. Her performance in the final has, in many ways, redefined the narrative of what it means to be a champion in today's competitive landscape—one where dedication, innovation, and resilience are as celebrated as the trophies that adorn the winners' stands.

Looking forward, the ramifications of this championship win are poised to extend far beyond the confines of one tournament. As the women's tennis circuit gears up for future challenges, there is a palpable sense of excitement and possibility. The strategic lessons learned from the final, the resilience shown throughout the tournament, and the overarching narrative of transformation all point towards a future where women's tennis continues to thrive. The landscape is evolving, and with it, the roles of established champions and emerging stars are being redefined. Barbora Krejčíková's win is a harbinger of this new era—a signal that the sport is ready to embrace change while honouring the rich traditions that have always made it so compelling.

In essence, the Women's Championship has provided a moment of reflection, celebration, and inspiration. It is a reminder that tennis is much more than a game of physical skill; it is an art form, a mental chess match, and a platform for stories of human endeavour. As we applaud Krejčíková's achievements and absorb the lessons from her journey, we are also invited to reimagine the future of women's tennis—a future where every match is an opportunity for innovation, every player a potential pioneer, and every champion a beacon of hope for the next generation.

Ultimately, this championship has not only crowned a winner but also set a benchmark for excellence in the sport. The lasting impact of Barbora Krejčíková's victory will be measured not only in titles and accolades but in the inspiration it provides to players and fans alike. As the echo of the final rally fades into history, the narrative of this Women's Championship will continue to resonate, fueling dreams and ambitions across the tennis world.

In celebrating the spirit of this remarkable tournament, we are reminded that every point played, every strategy devised, and every ounce of determination displayed on court contributes to a legacy that transcends the boundaries of sport. The Women's Championship of this year has been a vivid demonstration of what can be achieved when talent meets tenacity, and it is this legacy that will undoubtedly shape the future of women's tennis for generations to come.

With Barbora Krejčíková's championship win now firmly etched in the annals of tennis history, we stand on the threshold of a new chapter—one where the lessons of the past are seamlessly integrated with the promise of tomorrow. The journey has been long and hard-fought, marked by moments of brilliance and bouts of adversity, yet it is this very journey that has enriched the sport and elevated it to its current stature. As we look back on the championship and gaze forward to the challenges ahead, one thing remains clear: the future of women's tennis is brighter than ever, and its potential is limitless.

In the end, the Women's Championship is a celebration of the human spirit, a testament to the power of perseverance, and a clear signal that while champions may come and go, the legacy they create endures. It is a story that will continue to inspire, to challenge, and to enthral—reminding us all why we love this beautiful game.

Novak Djokovic

Carlos Alcaraz

Iga Swiatek

Ons Jabeur

The Men's Championship

In a tournament defined by its high drama and relentless pursuit of perfection, the 2024 Men's Championship has once again delivered a spectacle for the ages. At the centre of this enthralling narrative stands Carlos Alcaraz, whose victory has not only cemented his place among the elite of men's tennis but also sparked intense discussions about the future of the sport. From his early days on the circuit to the climax of the final match, Alcaraz's journey has been a masterclass in athletic prowess, mental toughness, and the ever-evolving art of tennis. As we dissect the final match in comprehensive detail and examine its broader significance, it becomes clear that this championship is more than just a tournament—it is a turning point in the legacy of a champion and a harbinger for the future dynamics of men's tennis.

It is impossible to overstate the magnitude of Alcaraz's achievement. Emerging from a field of fierce competitors, the young Spaniard has shown time and again that his talent transcends mere potential. His triumph in 2024, following a series of impressive performances throughout the tournament, represents not only a personal victory but a symbolic passing of the torch in an era where speed, agility, and strategic innovation are paramount. Alcaraz's journey has been one of perseverance and evolution, with every match serving as a stepping stone that refined his game and steeled his resolve.

The final match was a veritable rollercoaster of emotion and technical brilliance—a battle that unfolded with the precision of a well-rehearsed symphony and the unpredictability of a live drama. From the very first serve, it was clear that this was a contest where every point carried immense weight. The atmosphere on Centre Court was electric, with fans on the edge of their seats, fully aware that they were about to witness a clash of titans. Alcaraz's opponent, a seasoned competitor known for his resilience and tactical acumen, proved to be a formidable adversary. The match was a seesaw of momentum, punctuated by breathtaking rallies and moments where the outcome hung in the balance with each shot.

Throughout the contest, Alcaraz demonstrated a maturity and tactical intelligence that belied his years. His serve, a weapon honed through countless hours of practice, was as effective as it was unpredictable. He mixed power with precision, often catching his opponent off guard with well-placed deliveries that seemed to defy the laws of physics. But it wasn't just his serving that set him apart. His movement on the court was a blend of grace and explosive speed—each step and pivot executed with the assurance of a player who has mastered his craft. The final was a vivid illustration of his ability to transition seamlessly from defence to attack, utilising an array of shots that ranged from blistering forehands to delicate drop shots that coaxed errors from his rival.

There were moments in the match that will be etched in the memories of tennis fans for years to come. At one point, with the score finely poised and the tension palpable, Alcaraz unleashed a sequence of rapid-fire returns that shifted the momentum decisively in his favour. Each stroke was a testament to his unwavering focus, as he anticipated every move and responded with the clarity of a chess grandmaster planning his next strategy. His opponent, despite his experience and formidable record, seemed unable to keep pace with the sheer dynamism of Alcaraz's play. Yet, the match was far from one-sided. There were stretches when the veteran rallied back, showcasing his own storied experience and reminding everyone that in tennis, every point is a battle and every rally a chance to seize control.

The significance of this final extends far beyond the scoreline. In analysing the match, one is struck by the nuances of strategy that unfolded on the court. Alcaraz's game plan was meticulously crafted; he played not only to his strengths but also to expose the weaknesses of his opponent. His use of angles, his decision to vary the pace and spin on the ball, and his exceptional shot selection all converged to create a performance that was both aggressive and measured. There was an almost poetic quality to the way he constructed points, as if each play was part of a larger narrative that he was writing in real time. The match was a microcosm of modern tennis—an intricate dance of power, finesse, and psychological warfare.

Beyond the tactical brilliance displayed in the final, there is an entire narrative surrounding Carlos Alcaraz's legacy that is now being redefined. His victory in 2024 is not just another trophy added to his cabinet—it is a moment that encapsulates the journey of a young champion rising to the top in a sport where longevity and consistency have long been the hallmarks of greatness. Alcaraz's narrative is one of rapid evolution; within a relatively short span, he has transformed from a promising talent into a player whose every match is dissected by pundits and admired by fans worldwide. His triumph in the final serves as a declaration that the future of men's tennis is in safe hands, with a player who is not only willing to push the boundaries of what is possible on the court but is also capable of inspiring a new generation of tennis enthusiasts.

The legacy considerations of Alcaraz's win are multifaceted. For one, his championship victory represents a significant milestone in the ongoing shift in power dynamics within the men's game. For decades, the sport has been dominated by a handful of legendary figures whose careers spanned over many years. Alcaraz's rise, characterised by a blend of youthful exuberance and tactical intelligence, signals a new era where the mantle of leadership is passed on with a fresh sense of urgency and innovation. His win is not only a testament to his own abilities but also a reflection of the evolving landscape of tennis, where technological advancements, enhanced training methods, and a deeper understanding of sports science are reshaping the competitive arena.

There is also a broader cultural impact to consider. Alcaraz's championship has already sparked conversations about what it means to be a modern tennis champion. His style of play, marked by both flair and an unyielding work ethic, resonates with fans across the globe, transcending the sport itself and influencing popular culture. In locker rooms, on social media, and across media outlets, the buzz around his victory has ignited debates about the future of tennis. Many see in him a reflection of the modern athlete—one who is as comfortable in the digital age as he is on the grass courts of Wimbledon. His journey is being celebrated not only as an individual achievement but as a symbol of progress, a beacon of hope that the next generation of players can rise to the challenge and carry forward the legacy of excellence in men's tennis.

The final match also had significant implications for the broader dynamics of men's tennis. With each rally and every strategic adjustment, the game is evolving in response to the new realities of the modern era. Analysts are already pointing to the final as a turning point—a match that encapsulated the transition from an era defined by sheer physical endurance to one where mental agility and strategic planning are increasingly decisive. Alcaraz's performance has raised the bar for his contemporaries, forcing them to reconsider their own approaches and prompting a renewed focus on versatility and adaptability. It is not merely about winning points; it is about winning minds, reading the game, and executing under pressure. This paradigm shift is likely to have far-reaching effects on how players train, how coaches design strategies, and even how tournaments are structured in the future.

For the fans, the excitement surrounding Alcaraz's win is palpable. The final was a rollercoaster of emotions—a match that saw heartbreak and jubilation, frustration and elation, often in the span of a few moments. Every serve, every volley, and every break of serve contributed to a narrative that was as compelling as any story in literature. There were instances when the collective heartbeat of the crowd seemed to synchronise with the pace of the match, each point eliciting gasps, cheers, and a sense of shared destiny. In these moments, the sport transcended the boundaries of competition and became a communal experience—a celebration of the human spirit, the thrill of risk, and the beauty of perseverance.

Carlos Alcaraz's narrative is also one of personal growth—a journey marked by challenges that have only served to strengthen his resolve. Throughout the tournament, he faced setbacks and moments of doubt, yet each obstacle became a stepping stone toward his ultimate triumph. His ability to bounce back from adversity, to adapt his game in the face of unexpected challenges, and to maintain an unwavering focus on his goal is a lesson in resilience that resonates far beyond the confines of tennis. In interviews following the final, Alcaraz spoke candidly about the struggles he faced and the mental battles he fought, offering a glimpse into the inner workings of a champion's mind. His humility, combined with an intense drive to succeed, has endeared him to fans and earned him the respect of his peers.

Moreover, the implications of this championship win extend to the global stage. As men's tennis continues to evolve, the influence of a champion like Alcaraz cannot be overstated. His victory has the potential to redefine rivalries, reshape tournament narratives, and even influence the next generation of tennis players. In academies and training centres across the world, young aspirants will look to his journey as a blueprint for success—a model that emphasises not only physical prowess but also mental strength, strategic thinking, and the courage to innovate. His style of play, characterised by a blend of aggressive shot-making and thoughtful shot selection, is already inspiring a wave of coaching innovations and training techniques designed to replicate his success. In this way, his championship win is not just a personal triumph—it is a catalyst for change that could transform the landscape of men's tennis for years to come.

The legacy of Carlos Alcaraz's victory is also intricately linked to the broader evolution of the sport itself. In an era where technology and data analytics are becoming integral to competitive strategy, the final served as a showcase for the modern athlete. Alcaraz's performance highlighted the importance of adaptability—the ability to learn from every encounter and to fine-tune one's game in response to evolving challenges. This new breed of tennis champion is not defined solely by physical attributes but by an intellectual approach to the game that values innovation as much as tradition. As the sport continues to embrace new technologies, from advanced training regimens to real-time match analytics, the skills demonstrated by Alcaraz are likely to become the new benchmark for success.

There is also a deeper, more philosophical dimension to this championship. At its core, the final was a reminder that tennis, like life, is a series of challenges and triumphs—a delicate balance between victory and defeat, success and failure. In every match, the players are not just contesting for titles; they are writing their own stories, filled with moments of brilliance, instances of vulnerability, and the relentless pursuit of excellence. Alcaraz's win is a powerful reminder that every setback is an opportunity for growth, that every challenge is a chance to evolve, and that the true measure of a champion lies not in the trophies they collect, but in the legacy they leave behind.

As we look to the future, the impact of this championship will undoubtedly reverberate throughout the world of men's tennis. The final has set in motion a series of changes that will influence everything from player development to tactical innovation. It is a call to arms for the next generation of players—a challenge to rise to the occasion, to push the boundaries of what is possible, and to embrace the evolving dynamics of a sport that is as unpredictable as it is inspiring. The message is clear: the future of men's tennis belongs to those who are willing to adapt, to innovate, and to carry forward the torch of excellence with a blend of passion, intelligence, and unwavering determination.

In the wake of Alcaraz's victory, discussions about the future of the sport are more fervent than ever. Analysts and enthusiasts alike are pondering the ripple effects of his win—how it will influence the dynamics of rivalries, the strategies employed by top players, and even the way tournaments are conducted. It is an exciting time for tennis, one where the convergence of tradition and modernity is creating new narratives that promise to captivate fans for decades to come. The championship has opened up a dialogue about the nature of competition in the 21st century—a dialogue that encompasses not only the physical and technical aspects of the game but also the mental and emotional dimensions that make tennis such a compelling spectacle.

In conclusion, the 2024 Men's Championship will be remembered as a defining moment in the annals of tennis history—a moment when a young champion, Carlos Alcaraz, not only demonstrated the brilliance of his game but also redefined the future trajectory of men's tennis.

The final match was a microcosm of modern sport: a blend of raw athleticism, strategic ingenuity, and the indomitable human spirit. Alcaraz's journey, from the early rounds to the dramatic climax on Centre Court, is a testament to the relentless pursuit of excellence—a narrative that inspires, challenges, and transforms the way we view the sport.

His victory is not merely a personal triumph but a signal of the times—a clear indication that the future of men's tennis is bright, dynamic, and full of promise. As players, coaches, and fans alike digest the lessons of the final, one thing is certain: the legacy of this championship will shape the game for years to come, influencing everything from training methodologies to the very ethos of competition. In the ever-changing landscape of men's tennis, Carlos Alcaraz has emerged as a beacon of hope, a symbol of progress, and a reminder that every match is an opportunity to redefine what it means to be a champion.

So, as we celebrate this monumental victory and anticipate the challenges and triumphs that lie ahead, we do so with the understanding that the spirit of tennis is alive and well—embodied in every swing, every serve, and every moment of brilliance that graces the court. The 2024 Men's Championship is more than a title; it is a statement of intent, a declaration that the future is here, and it is being written by those who dare to dream, to fight, and to inspire. And in that spirit, the legacy of Carlos Alcaraz will continue to grow, leaving an indelible mark on the world of tennis and lighting the way for generations of champions to come.

Disability Tennis at Wimbledon

Wimbledon has always been a stage where the best of tennis come together to produce moments of magic and passion, and in recent years, the spotlight has shone even brighter on disability tennis. This year's tournament has not only celebrated the tradition and glamour of the All England Club but has also served as a vibrant platform for showcasing the evolution, talent, and undeniable spirit of wheelchair and quad events. Over the years, disability tennis at Wimbledon has grown from a modest inclusion to an essential part of the Championships' fabric, capturing the hearts of fans worldwide with its breathtaking athleticism, fierce competition, and stories of determination that transcend the boundaries of the sport.

From its early days, disability tennis has steadily evolved, finding its rightful place alongside the able-bodied competitions. The integration of wheelchair and quad events at Wimbledon stands as a testament to the tournament's commitment to inclusivity and excellence. What was once viewed as a niche segment of the sport has blossomed into a global phenomenon. The events not only highlight the incredible skill and athleticism of the players but also underscore a broader message: that tennis, in all its forms, is for everyone. With cutting-edge training techniques, improved equipment, and an ever-increasing support network, disability tennis has grown leaps and bounds, drawing in a diverse audience and inspiring young athletes across the globe.

The importance of disability tennis on the global stage cannot be overstated. As more fans tune in and as media coverage expands, the stories of these athletes resonate far beyond the courts of Wimbledon. Their journeys—fraught with challenges, marked by perseverance, and celebrated with triumphant victories—serve as powerful reminders of the human spirit's resilience. The visibility of disability tennis at a venue as prestigious as Wimbledon sends a strong, affirmative message to the world: that every athlete, regardless of physical ability, deserves recognition and the opportunity to shine on the biggest stage.

2024 saw a host of exceptional performances that not only elevated the standard of play but also redefined what is possible in disability tennis. In the men's wheelchair singles, Alfie Hewett once again proved why he is a force to be reckoned with. His clinical precision, combined with an instinctive understanding of the game, allowed him to outplay his competitors and secure a well-deserved title. Alfie's journey in 2024 has been a rollercoaster of emotion, with moments of breathtaking brilliance and bouts of intense determination that kept fans on the edge of their seats. His ability to read the game and his relentless drive have cemented his reputation as one of the sport's leading lights, and his triumph this past year is celebrated as much for his skill as it is for the inspiration he provides to aspiring athletes.

On the women's side, Diede de Groot has continued to dominate, affirming her status as one of the greatest in the history of wheelchair tennis. Her performances this season have been nothing short of extraordinary. With her powerful strokes, agile manoeuvres, and a tactical acumen that borders on the genius, Diede has not only reclaimed her crown but also pushed the envelope of what is expected in high-stakes competition. The women's wheelchair singles final was a masterclass in athleticism and mental strength, and Diede's victory resonated deeply with fans who see her as a role model in every sense of the word.

The quad singles competition, too, has grown in stature and intensity. Niels Vink, whose name has become synonymous with excellence in quad tennis, delivered performances that left no doubt about his capabilities. His triumph in the quad singles event in 2024 has been a testament to years of hard work, innovation, and sheer determination. The way he navigated the challenges on the court, adapting his strategy in real time and executing plays with surgical precision, spoke volumes about his dedication to his craft. For many, Niels Vink's journey has been a source of inspiration—a reminder that obstacles can be overcome with the right blend of grit and ingenuity.

Doubles events have also provided some of the most enthralling moments of the tournament. In the men's wheelchair doubles, the pairing of Alfie Hewett and Gordon Reid has long been regarded as a formidable duo, and their 2024 performance only reinforced that reputation. Their synergy on the court, the seamless transitions, and the almost telepathic coordination they exhibited during critical points made them a joy to watch. The way they shared responsibilities and covered for each other on the court was a masterclass in teamwork and trust—qualities that have become the hallmark of successful doubles partnerships.

Similarly, in the women's wheelchair doubles, the combination of Yui Kamiji and Kgothatso Montjane produced magic on the grass. Their game was a blend of speed, strategy, and an intuitive understanding of each other's play that allowed them to overcome even the most daunting challenges. Their partnership is celebrated not only for its technical brilliance but also for the emotional connection and respect that underpins every match they play. For fans, watching Kamiji and Montjane in action is a reminder of the power of collaboration and the beauty that emerges when talent and teamwork intersect.

The quad doubles event, featuring the dynamic duo of Sam Schröder and Niels Vink, has quickly become a fan favourite. Their matches are characterised by fast-paced exchanges, daring shot selections, and a palpable sense of camaraderie that elevates the spectacle to new heights. The energy they bring to the court is infectious, igniting cheers and applause from the stands and beyond. Their success in 2024 has not only added to the legacy of disability tennis but has also set the stage for an even brighter future, where these events continue to captivate audiences and inspire a new generation of athletes.

Looking ahead to the 2025 tournament, the narrative of disability tennis at Wimbledon promises even more excitement and innovation. The upcoming Championships are set to feature key matches that could redefine emerging storylines in the sport. With a blend of seasoned champions and rising stars ready to make their mark, the competition is poised to be as unpredictable as it is thrilling. New talents are emerging from training academies and local clubs across the globe, eager to write their own chapters in the rich history of disability tennis. These young athletes bring with them fresh perspectives, unbridled energy, and the potential to upset established hierarchies, making every match a tantalising glimpse into the future of the sport.

The 2025 tournament will undoubtedly highlight several memorable moments that will be talked about for years to come. Key matches are expected to be filled with dramatic shifts in momentum, daring plays, and the kind of resilient spirit that defines Wimbledon. Each game is not merely a contest of points but a narrative of individual journeys, where players overcome personal and physical challenges to achieve greatness. These moments, whether they are breathtaking rallies that stretch to the final point or strategic masterstrokes that turn the tide of a match, add layers of depth and excitement to the broader Wimbledon narrative.

Profiles of standout players and their journeys are set to take centre stage as well. In-depth features on athletes like Alfie Hewett, Diede de Groot, Niels Vink, and others will provide fans with a closer look at the personal stories behind the phenomenal on-court performances. These profiles are more than just sports journalism—they are powerful stories of determination, resilience, and passion. They remind us that behind every medal and every trophy lies a journey filled with ups and downs, setbacks and comebacks, all of which culminate in the pursuit of excellence. The players' stories resonate on a personal level, inspiring countless fans and aspiring athletes who see in them the embodiment of what it means to overcome adversity.

Disability tennis has also had a significant impact on the broader Wimbledon narrative, enriching the tournament's tapestry with themes of inclusivity and empowerment. The integration of wheelchair and quad events has broadened the appeal of Wimbledon, inviting a more diverse audience to partake in the celebration of tennis. Fans are not just coming for the glamour and tradition of the Championships; they are also drawn by the sheer human drama that unfolds on the court in these events. The electrifying atmosphere created by the supporters, the passionate cheers, and the undeniable sense of community that surrounds disability tennis all contribute to a narrative that is as moving as it is competitive.

Moreover, the growing prominence of disability tennis has had a ripple effect on the global stage. As the events receive more media coverage and sponsorship, they are becoming increasingly influential in shaping perceptions of what is possible in sport. The visibility of these athletes and their remarkable achievements sends a clear message: that sport is for everyone, regardless of physical challenges. This message resonates deeply in an era that champions diversity, inclusion, and equal opportunity. The growth of disability tennis is not just a triumph for the athletes—it is a victory for the sport as a whole, paving the way for future generations of players who might have once been overlooked.

The narratives emerging from disability tennis at Wimbledon also serve as powerful tools for advocacy and social change. By bringing the stories of these athletes into the mainstream, Wimbledon is helping to challenge stereotypes and break down barriers. The success and determination of players like Hewett, de Groot, Vink, Kamiji, Montjane, Schröder, and their partners inspire not only future tennis stars but also individuals facing challenges in everyday life. Their stories are a reminder that with the right support, unwavering determination, and a belief in oneself, obstacles can be overcome. In this way, disability tennis becomes much more than a competitive event—it becomes a beacon of hope and a catalyst for positive change in society.

As we approach Wimbledon 2025, the tournament's organisers are committed to building on this legacy and continuing to elevate the profile of disability tennis. Plans for enhanced facilities, improved accessibility, and even more robust media coverage are all part of a broader strategy to ensure that every aspect of the tournament reflects the values of inclusivity and excellence. These initiatives are designed to create an environment where every athlete can perform at their best, where fans can enjoy the full spectrum of tennis excellence, and where the stories of triumph and perseverance are shared with the world.

Looking to the future, one can only be excited about the potential for disability tennis to influence the sport on a global scale. With each passing year, the level of competition rises, new talents emerge, and the overall quality of play continues to improve. The impact of these changes is already being felt in training methodologies, equipment design, and even the way matches are broadcast and analysed. Disability tennis is evolving at a rapid pace, and Wimbledon is at the forefront of this transformation, serving as both a stage and a catalyst for innovation.

In conclusion, the story of disability tennis at Wimbledon is a vibrant tapestry woven from threads of resilience, passion, and groundbreaking achievement. From the early days of integration to the dazzling performances of the 2024 champions, the journey has been marked by both triumph and transformation. The narratives of Alfie Hewett, Diede de Groot, Niels Vink, Yui Kamiji, Kgothatso Montjane, Sam Schröder, and their partners are a testament to what can be achieved when talent meets opportunity, and when the spirit of the game is allowed to flourish in an inclusive and supportive environment.

As we look forward to the 2025 Championships, disability tennis promises to deliver even more unforgettable moments, inspiring stories, and competitive brilliance. It is a celebration of not only the sport itself but also the incredible individuals who push boundaries, defy expectations, and redefine what it means to be a champion. With every match played and every point won, disability tennis at Wimbledon continues to shape a legacy that will inspire future generations of players and fans alike.

In this remarkable chapter of Wimbledon's history, disability tennis stands tall as a beacon of progress and a celebration of human achievement. It reminds us that the true spirit of sport lies not in perfection but in the courage to face challenges head-on, the determination to keep fighting, and the unyielding belief that every athlete deserves a chance to shine. And as the grass courts prepare to welcome another season of fierce competition and heartfelt stories, one thing is certain: disability tennis will continue to be an integral part of Wimbledon's legacy, a legacy that honours tradition while boldly embracing the promise of tomorrow.

Doubles and Mixed Doubles

Wimbledon has always been a tournament where tradition meets innovation, and nowhere is that more evident than in the doubles and mixed doubles events. These competitions offer a refreshing twist to the main draw, bringing together a blend of strategy, camaraderie, and sheer athleticism that enrich the overall Wimbledon experience. In 2024, the tournament witnessed some truly spectacular doubles performances. Harri Heliövaara and Henry Patten stunned the crowds in the men's doubles, while Kateřina Siniaková and Taylor Townsend dazzled in the women's doubles. In the mixed doubles, Jan Zieliński and Hsieh Su-wei emerged as the champions, showcasing a delightful mix of precision and creativity. As we look ahead to the 2025 tournament, there's plenty to be excited about—not only in terms of new partnerships and emerging talents but also in the way the doubles format continues to evolve and add a unique flavour to Wimbledon.

It all started with a season of surprises and spectacular displays of teamwork. Harri Heliövaara and Henry Patten's triumph in the men's doubles was a masterclass in tactical brilliance and on-court chemistry. Their journey through the 2024 Championships was marked by a series of well-orchestrated plays and nerve-wracking matches that kept fans glued to their seats. Both players, known for their exceptional reflexes and court awareness, seemed to understand intuitively how to cover each other's weaknesses. Their partnership was built on trust and shared determination, with each point won a testament to countless hours of training and an unyielding focus on perfection. Their performance wasn't just about power or speed—it was about making the right decisions at crucial moments, whether it was a perfectly timed net play or a calculated lunge to retrieve a difficult shot.

Meanwhile, in the women's doubles, Kateřina Siniaková and Taylor Townsend delivered a performance that was both elegant and aggressive. Siniaková, with her superb baseline consistency and fluid movement, combined with Townsend's dynamic attacking style, created a partnership that was greater than the sum of its parts. Their matches were characterised by crisp volleys and a deep understanding of each other's rhythm. Fans were treated to rallies that seemed to blend art and athleticism, as the pair used their complementary skills to dismantle even the toughest opponents. Their success was a reminder that doubles isn't simply about pairing two talented players—it's about the seamless fusion of their styles, where communication and mutual support can turn potential pitfalls into opportunities for spectacular play.

Not to be outdone, the mixed doubles champions, Jan Zieliński and Hsieh Su-wei, carved out a niche for themselves with a performance that was both inventive and unpredictable. Mixed doubles has always been a bit of a wild card at Wimbledon, where the combination of male and female playing styles produces matches full of surprises. Zieliński and Hsieh showcased a remarkable synergy that few partnerships can claim. Hsieh's quick thinking and deft touch at the net complemented Zieliński's power and consistency from the baseline, making their matches a joy to watch. Their game plan was built on adaptability—switching tactics seamlessly as the match evolved, reading their opponents' movements, and countering with a mix of power and finesse that left little room for error.

As we look to the 2025 tournament, it's clear that the doubles scene is only going to get more exciting. The new season is brimming with emerging talents and intriguing new partnerships, and there's a renewed focus on strategy that is set to transform the doubles court into a battleground of wits and reflexes. Analysts are already talking about how the evolution of doubles tactics in recent years has changed the way matches are played. No longer is doubles simply a game of quick exchanges at the net; it has evolved into a sophisticated contest of positioning, timing, and strategic shot selection.

One of the key factors driving this evolution is the increasing use of data analytics and video analysis. Coaches and players now have access to detailed breakdowns of opponents' serve patterns, preferred court positions, and even the slightest nuances in movement. This has allowed teams to develop bespoke strategies tailored to counter specific threats. In 2024, we saw several teams adjust their formations mid-match, switching from a traditional side-by-side formation to a more dynamic, rotated system that caught their opponents off guard. These tactical shifts often made the difference in tight matches, where every point could swing momentum and dictate the outcome.

The 2025 tournament is expected to further this trend, with doubles teams leveraging technology to fine-tune their approaches. For example, we might see teams adopt more aggressive net play, capitalising on quicker reflexes and innovative formations designed to exploit the gaps in their opponents' coverage. There's also an emerging trend of hybrid strategies—teams that can seamlessly blend baseline consistency with net aggression. Such flexibility is critical in a game that is as much about mental agility as it is about physical prowess. It is this very adaptability that often separates the champions from the rest of the pack.

Beyond the tactics and technical prowess, doubles and mixed doubles have a special place in the Wimbledon experience because they capture the essence of the sport in a different light. The doubles format brings an element of unpredictability and spontaneity that is sometimes less apparent in singles play. The rapid-fire exchanges, the strategic poaching at the net, and the intricate dance of movement and communication all combine to create a spectacle that is both thrilling and deeply engaging. For many fans, watching doubles is a reminder of why tennis is such a beloved sport—a celebration of teamwork, creativity, and the sheer joy of the game.

The partnership dynamics in doubles are particularly fascinating. Take, for instance, the way in which established pairs like Heliövaara and Patten have honed their instincts over years of playing together. Their ability to anticipate each other's moves is almost telepathic, and it is this unspoken understanding that often leaves opponents scrambling. In contrast, newer pairings, such as those emerging on the women's circuit, are still in the process of building that kind of rapport. The 2025 Championships could well be a proving ground for these new partnerships, where early-season chemistry is tested under the pressure of Wimbledon's storied atmosphere.

It's also worth noting how doubles play has a profound impact on the overall culture of Wimbledon. The doubles matches, with their emphasis on flair and fast-paced action, bring a different energy to the tournament. They are a reminder that tennis is not just a solitary endeavour but a sport that thrives on collaboration and mutual support. For the spectators, doubles offers a refreshing alternative to the high-intensity drama of singles matches—a chance to appreciate the nuances of teamwork, strategy, and the collective spirit of the game.

In addition, mixed doubles add an extra layer of intrigue. The very nature of combining male and female athletes in a high-pressure competitive setting offers a unique perspective on the game. Mixed doubles require a delicate balance—each player must not only excel individually but also complement their partner's strengths and mitigate any weaknesses. This dual responsibility often results in matches that are as tactically complex as they are entertaining. The 2024 mixed doubles champions, Zieliński and Hsieh, epitomised this balance. Their ability to alternate between offensive and defensive play, coupled with a seemingly innate understanding of each other's rhythms, set a high standard for what mixed doubles can achieve. Their success has sparked conversations about how mixed doubles might evolve in the coming years, especially as more emphasis is placed on dynamic, inter-gender partnerships that challenge traditional roles and expectations.

Looking ahead to 2025, the doubles events promise to be a crucible of innovation and talent. There will be new faces, unexpected alliances, and moments of sheer brilliance that will redefine how we perceive doubles tennis. Emerging players, eager to make their mark, are already studying the strategies of the great teams of 2024. They are learning that success in doubles isn't merely about individual prowess—it's about synchronisation, adaptability, and the willingness to take calculated risks. As the sport continues to evolve, doubles will likely become even more central to Wimbledon's identity, offering fans an ever-changing canvas of tactical ingenuity and spirited competition.

Moreover, the role of doubles in enriching the Wimbledon experience extends beyond the technical and tactical aspects. It has a profound cultural resonance. Doubles matches are often characterised by moments of humour, unexpected brilliance, and a shared sense of camaraderie that can make the tension of big matches feel more relaxed and festive. There's something undeniably charming about seeing two athletes coordinate their efforts on the court, celebrating each point with high-fives, knowing smiles, or even a quick nod of mutual respect. These moments contribute to a festive atmosphere that is uniquely Wimbledon—where every match, every set, and every point is a celebration of the sport's rich tradition and innovative future.

The beauty of doubles and mixed doubles is that they remind us that tennis is as much a team sport as it is an individual pursuit. For decades, Wimbledon has celebrated the heroics of solo champions, but the doubles format has steadily gained recognition for its own brand of excitement and skill. The narrative of Wimbledon is incomplete without the stories that emerge from these matches—the underdog teams that overcome staggering odds, the veteran pairs that prove there's still plenty of fight left in them, and the rising stars who bring fresh energy and creative play to the court. These narratives are woven into the fabric of the tournament, creating a rich tapestry of moments that resonate with fans long after the final point has been played.

As we reflect on the achievements of the 2024 Champions and look forward to what 2025 has in store, it is clear that doubles tennis is evolving into a vital pillar of the Wimbledon experience. Whether it's the seamless coordination of Harri Heliövaara and Henry Patten in the men's doubles, the graceful yet powerful interplay between Kateřina Siniaková and Taylor Townsend in the women's doubles, or the inventive spark of mixed doubles champions Jan Zieliński and Hsieh Su-wei, each victory adds a new chapter to the grand narrative of Wimbledon. Their successes are not just isolated moments of triumph but part of a larger, ongoing story that celebrates diversity in playing styles, the fusion of tradition with modernity, and the unyielding passion for tennis.

In the coming years, as new strategies are developed, new partnerships formed, and new challenges met head-on, doubles and mixed doubles will continue to provide a refreshing counterpoint to the intensity of singles competition. They remind us that behind every brilliant serve or thunderous volley lies a story of teamwork, dedication, and the unbreakable bonds forged on the court. For fans, these matches are a testament to the beauty of collaboration and the thrill of unexpected chemistry—a celebration of the fact that sometimes, the best results come when two minds, and hearts, work in unison.

Ultimately, doubles and mixed doubles are more than just additional events at Wimbledon—they are integral to the tournament's soul. They add layers of excitement and nuance to the Championships, enhancing its global appeal and reinforcing its status as a bastion of tennis excellence. As we look to the future, it's exciting to imagine how these events will continue to evolve, bringing new stories, innovative strategies, and unforgettable moments that will capture the imaginations of fans around the world.

In essence, the doubles format encapsulates the spirit of Wimbledon—where tradition meets innovation, where individual brilliance is celebrated within the context of teamwork, and where every match is a microcosm of the larger, ever-evolving narrative of tennis. With the 2024 Champions setting high standards and the promise of even more thrilling contests in 2025, doubles and mixed doubles will undoubtedly remain at the heart of Wimbledon's legacy—a legacy defined by shared passion, mutual respect, and the timeless joy of playing the game.

The Juniors and Future Stars

Wimbledon's junior tournaments have always been a breeding ground for the next generation of tennis legends, and this year was no exception. The energy and excitement emanating from the courts where emerging talents are honing their skills is palpable—a reminder that the future of tennis is in safe hands. At junior Wimbledon, every match is a story in the making, filled with promising serves, lightning-fast rallies, and moments that often hint at the brilliance that will later define the professional game.

This year's junior events showcased a cornucopia of emerging talents, each with a unique style and a determination that belies their age. These young players bring a refreshing mix of raw talent and fearless ambition to the courts, and the tournament has quickly become a magnet for fans who are eager to catch a glimpse of the stars of tomorrow. The atmosphere is electric, as coaches, family members, and tennis enthusiasts gather to witness these future champions in action. There's an almost magnetic pull to the junior matches, where every serve and volley is charged with the promise of greatness.

Notable matches throughout the junior rounds have been nothing short of inspirational. In one thrilling encounter, a fiercely competitive five-set battle kept spectators on the edge of their seats, as two players traded momentum like seasoned professionals. The young athletes exhibited remarkable composure under pressure—each point won or lost felt like a precursor to the intensity of a major final. Such matches not only captivate the audience but also serve as valuable learning experiences for the players themselves. The sheer resilience displayed by these juniors in the face of adversity is a testament to their potential, and it is moments like these that give a glimpse into the calibre of talent that will soon grace the professional tours.

Among the standout players to watch are a handful of prodigies whose performances have already generated buzz among tennis aficionados and pundits alike. One such rising star, with a powerful forehand and an unyielding work ethic, has already been tipped by many as a future Grand Slam contender. Equally impressive is a player known for an almost preternatural ability to read the game—displaying tactical awareness that is rare in someone so young. These players, and others like them, not only represent the next wave of tennis excellence but also embody the passion and dedication required to excel at the highest levels.

Junior Wimbledon is more than just a tournament; it's a proving ground—a crucible where dreams are tested, refined, and sometimes even shattered, only to be rebuilt stronger than before. Historically, many of today's top professionals made their first mark on the hallowed grass of Wimbledon as juniors. The tournament has a unique way of transforming raw potential into polished skill, acting as a springboard that launches careers. It is here that young players experience the pressures and rigours of competitive tennis in a setting steeped in tradition, a setting that ultimately prepares them for the challenges of the professional circuit.

The significance of junior Wimbledon cannot be overstated. For many budding players, it is the first real taste of life in the limelight—a chance to perform on a stage where even the smallest gesture is magnified and every mistake scrutinised. It is a trial by fire that not only tests their technical skills but also their mental fortitude. The lessons learned here, whether in handling pressure or developing a strategic game plan, often lay the foundation for future success. It's no exaggeration to say that junior Wimbledon is the first stepping stone in what could become a glittering career. For parents, coaches, and even casual observers, the tournament is a thrilling preview of what the future holds for tennis.

What's particularly remarkable about these junior events is the blend of passion and raw potential that is on full display. Unlike the seasoned professionals who have already experienced the highs and lows of the Grand Slam circuit, these young players are still exploring the boundaries of their talent. Their unbridled enthusiasm and willingness to experiment often lead to moments of unexpected brilliance. In one match, a daring drop shot that defied expectations and left the opponent scrambling for a response became the turning point that propelled a young contender into the next round. It is these unpredictable moments that remind us why junior Wimbledon is so essential—it's a microcosm of the sport's constant evolution, where innovation and tradition coexist on the same court.

THE JUNIORS AND FUTURE STARS

The ripple effects of these junior tournaments extend far beyond the immediate matches. Scouts, sponsors, and tennis academies from around the world keep a keen eye on the tournament, searching for that rare gem—a player with the potential to dominate the sport for years to come. For many juniors, performing well at Wimbledon can mean a significant boost in their careers, opening doors to professional training opportunities, sponsorships, and invitations to elite competitions. It's a high-stakes environment where every match is a chance to prove oneself not just to the present audience, but to the entire future landscape of tennis.

For the fans, junior Wimbledon offers a delightful mix of nostalgia and anticipation. There's something deeply moving about watching young athletes channel the same spirit and determination that once propelled their idols to greatness. The contrast between the unfiltered exuberance of youth and the refined mastery of seasoned professionals creates an inspiring narrative that resonates with viewers of all ages. It is a reminder that every champion was once a beginner, and that the journey to greatness is paved with persistence, passion, and an unyielding desire to succeed.

Looking ahead to future seasons, the impact of junior Wimbledon on the professional game is already evident. The tournament not only provides a platform for emerging talent but also influences trends in playing style, strategy, and even training methods. As these juniors transition into the senior circuit, they carry with them the lessons learned on these historic courts, often infusing the professional game with fresh ideas and innovative techniques. In this way, junior Wimbledon acts as a catalyst for change, continually revitalising the sport with new talent and a renewed sense of possibility.

In summary, the juniors and future stars at Wimbledon embody the very essence of what makes tennis such a captivating sport. Their journeys are filled with challenges, triumphs, and the kind of raw emotion that reminds us of the beauty and unpredictability of the game. Junior Wimbledon is not merely an event on the calendar; it is a celebration of youthful ambition, a showcase of emerging talent, and a vital stepping stone for the professional careers of tomorrow. As we cheer on these young athletes, we are not just witnessing the future of tennis—we are experiencing a vibrant tapestry of dreams in the making, each match a chapter in the ongoing story of the sport.

Men's World Rankings as of March 2025

As of March 17, 2025, the ATP men's singles rankings reflect the dynamic nature of professional tennis, showcasing a blend of seasoned champions and emerging talents. Below is an overview of the top 10 players, highlighting their nationalities, ages, and recent performances:

Men's Tennis ATP Rankings 2025

Men

Singles Rankings

RK	↑↓	NAME	POINTS	AGE
1	-	Jannik Sinner	11,330	23
2	-	Alexander Zverev	7,945	27
3	-	Carlos Alcaraz	6,910	21
4	-	Taylor Fritz	4,900	27
5	↑2	Novak Djokovic	3,860	37
6	↓1	Casper Ruud	3,855	26
7	↑7	Jack Draper	3,800	23
8	↓2	Daniil Medvedev	3,680	29
9	↓1	Andrey Rublev	3,440	27
10	↓1	Stefanos Tsitsipas	3,405	26

Jannik Sinner (Italy) – Age 23, 11,330 points

Sinner continues to dominate the ATP rankings with his consistent performances and remarkable skill set. His aggressive baseline play and mental fortitude have solidified his position at the pinnacle of men's tennis.

Alexander Zverev (Germany) – Age 27, 7,945 points

Zverev remains a formidable force on the tour, known for his powerful serve and baseline game. Despite facing challenges in clinching Grand Slam titles, his resilience keeps him among the elite.

Carlos Alcaraz (Spain) – Age 21, 6,910 points

At just 21, Alcaraz has rapidly ascended the rankings, showcasing a versatile game and exceptional athleticism. His recent performances have marked him as a future Grand Slam contender.

Taylor Fritz (USA) – Age 27, 4,900 points

Fritz's consistent showings and powerful baseline game have earned him a spot in the top five. His recent performances highlight his potential to challenge for major titles.

Novak Djokovic (Serbia) – Age 37, 3,860 points

The 24-time Grand Slam champion has shifted his focus from rankings to major titles as he approaches the twilight of his illustrious career. Despite this, his presence in the top five underscores his enduring excellence.

Casper Ruud (Norway) – Age 26, 3,855 points

Ruud's steady climb in the rankings is a testament to his consistent performances and adaptability across different surfaces. His tactical acumen continues to earn him accolades on the tour.

Jack Draper (Great Britain) – Age 23, 3,800 points

Draper's recent surge, highlighted by his maiden Masters 1000 title at Indian Wells, has propelled him into the top ten for the first time. His powerful serve and all-court game make him a player to watch.

Daniil Medvedev (Russia) – Age 29, 3,680 points

Known for his unorthodox playing style and mental toughness, Medvedev remains a consistent threat in any tournament. His strategic approach continues to challenge his opponents.

Andrey Rublev (Russia) – Age 27, 3,440 points

Rublev's explosive game and relentless energy have kept him within the top ten. His recent performances reflect his determination to break further into the upper echelons of the sport.

Stefanos Tsitsipas (Greece) – Age 26, 3,405 points

Tsitsipas's one-handed backhand and creative shot-making have made him a fan favorite. His recent form indicates a readiness to vie for the sport's most prestigious titles.

These rankings illustrate the evolving landscape of men's tennis, where emerging talents challenge established champions, promising thrilling contests in the tournaments ahead.

Women's Tennis WTA Rankings as of March 2025

As of March 17, 2025, the Women's Tennis Association (WTA) singles rankings showcase a compelling mix of seasoned champions and rising stars, reflecting the dynamic nature of women's tennis. Below is an overview of the top 10 players, highlighting their nationalities, ages, and recent performances:

Women's Tennis WTA Rankings 2025

Singles Rankings

RK	↑↓	NAME	POINTS	AGE
1	-	Aryna Sabalenka	9,606	26
2	-	Iga Swiatek	7,375	23
3	-	Coco Gauff	6,063	21
4	-	Jessica Pegula	5,361	31
5	-	Madison Keys	5,004	30
6	↑5	Mirra Andreeva	4,710	17
7	↓1	Jasmine Paolini	4,518	29
8	↓1	Elena Rybakina	4,448	25
9	-	Zheng Qinwen	3,985	22
10	↓2	Emma Navarro	3,859	23

Aryna Sabalenka (Belarus) – Age 26, 9,606 points

Sabalenka continues to lead the WTA rankings, demonstrating her powerful game and consistency on the tour. Her aggressive baseline play and formidable serve make her a dominant force in women's tennis.

Iga Świątek (Poland) – Age 23, 7,375 points

Świątek maintains her position near the top with her exceptional clay-court prowess and strategic play. Her recent performances have solidified her reputation as a versatile and resilient competitor.

Coco Gauff (USA) – Age 21, 6,063 points
At just 21, Gauff has firmly established herself among the elite. Her athleticism, coupled with a mature on-court demeanor, continues to impress as she competes at the highest levels.

Jessica Pegula (USA) – Age 31, 5,361 points
Pegula's consistent performances and tactical intelligence have kept her in the upper echelons of the rankings. Her ability to adapt to different opponents and surfaces underscores her experience and skill.

Madison Keys (USA) – Age 30, 5,004 points
Known for her powerful groundstrokes and aggressive style, Keys remains a formidable presence on the tour. Her recent semifinal appearance at Indian Wells highlights her enduring competitiveness.

Mirra Andreeva (Russia) – Age 17, 4,710 points
The 17-year-old sensation has made a meteoric rise, capturing titles at both the Dubai Open and Indian Wells. Andreeva's victories over top-ranked players have marked her as one of the most promising talents in women's tennis.

Jasmine Paolini (Italy) – Age 29, 4,518 points
Paolini's steady ascent in the rankings is a testament to her perseverance and skill. Her recent performances reflect her growing confidence and capability to challenge higher-ranked opponents.

Elena Rybakina (Kazakhstan) – Age 25, 4,448 points
Rybakina's powerful serve and aggressive playstyle have kept her within the top ten. Her ability to perform on big stages continues to make her a player to watch.

Zheng Qinwen (China) – Age 22, 3,985 points
Zheng's impressive performances have propelled her into the top ten. Her agility and tactical approach have earned her significant victories and recognition on the tour.

Emma Navarro (USA) – Age 23, 3,859 points
Navarro's recent successes have seen her break into the top ten. Her consistent play and determination signal a bright future ahead.

These rankings highlight the evolving landscape of women's tennis, where emerging talents like Mirra Andreeva are making significant strides alongside established stars, promising an exciting season ahead.

Printed in Great Britain
by Amazon